How to Grow
HOUSE
PLANTS

By the Sunset Editorial Staff

Book Editor: Barbara Pesch

Lane Books · Menlo Park, California

FOREWORD

In an age of speed and its accompanying pressures, rewarding pleasures can come from simple things—a single flower in a vase, a blooming plant on the coffee table, or a window-sill array of African violets. The world of nature offers beauties to the eye even in small measures. An indoor plant of any sort can be enjoyed in only a few seconds of leisure and appreciated to its fullest, while an outdoor garden is seldom viewed with attention to intricate detail.

With these thoughts in mind the editors of *Sunset* have compiled this book for those who have grown some house plants and wish to grow more, and for the person who has just purchased or received a "first" plant and doesn't know how to care for it. The book is not intended to be a complete encyclopedia of house plants, but rather a handbook to be used as you garden.

The book is divided into sections in which the culture of each particular type of plant is discussed in detail. Charts, photographs, and art work have been employed to make the book as useful as possible.

It is our hope that this book will lead you farther into the fascinating world of growing plants within your home—that you will be challenged and enchanted, delighted and never dismayed.

COVER: Large expanse of glass provides ideal setting for indoor plants. In the photograph here you see Monstera deliciosa *trained on a pole, an azalea covered with a brilliant mass of red flowers, and a small pot of 'Hahn's Self-branching' ivy on the table. Several patio plants are visible through the window. Photograph by Jack McDowell.*

Executive Editor, Sunset Books: David E. Clark

Sixteenth Printing March 1974

CONTENTS

SPECIAL FEATURES

AN INTRODUCTION TO INDOOR GARDENING

Plants grown indoors are personal things. They are close to the eye and the touch and give you an intimate look at nature. How you use them will also be a personal thing. This book is intended to give you some ideas for the display of house plants to add to your enjoyment of them and success in growing them in your home.

Architects and interior designers have demonstrated the design value of plants incorporated in houses and places of business. Design schemes often include permanent planters or specify the use of plants in prescribed areas.

Indoor plants are no longer talked about in terms of color alone but are appraised for their form and texture. They are used in compositions. They can be bold and cast dramatic shadows or reflections or repeat outdoor forms, carrying the outdoors in and the indoors out—a blending of the two.

Today's trend toward opening interior spaces to the outside, increased simplicity in architectural design, and a resulting starkness and often lack of warmth have brought about new interest in indoor plants. Home owners, architects, and interior designers are finding that additional light provides a wider scope for indoor gardening as well as discovering that plants are structural forms besides being colorful or beautiful objects.

But the design value of house plants is not limited to the modern decor of new homes or office buildings. In old and new houses alike, the dish garden, the portable or built-in planter, and all of the various containers of the florist shop and the nursery have become designs with foliage and blooming plants.

GERANIUMS growing in a bright south or east window benefit from morning sun. A temperature of 60° to 70° is best. There will be fewer blooms in winter.

The indoor gardener interested primarily in color, or just in the pleasure of watching plants grow, has actually gained by the increased interest in foliage plants. The suppliers of house plants, encouraged by increasing sales, have made available a wider selection of all types of plants. The lists of plants now available to be grown in the house are growing steadily—there is a wide range of color, form, and texture.

Your personal collection of plants will largely be determined by the growing conditions in your home as well as the dictates of personal choice. Natural light is an important factor in growing plants in the house. However, increased research and experience in growing plants under artificial light have created new indoor gardening possibilities. This aspect of indoor gardening is covered later in the book (see pages 84-87). Before plunging into purchase of plants that may or may not perform well for you, assess your environment from the standpoint of plants' needs. Then purchase a plant or plants that will do well in that environment.

Outdoor plants can make their own adjustments to compensate for faulty gardening. Roots spread out through the top layers of the soil when the lower layers become waterlogged, or they go deeper when the surface layers dry out. Plants grown indoors are dependent upon the grower. Their roots have no place to go. They must get along with the conditions of the soil within the container and with the food they find there.

These then are factors that must be taken into consideration before you try your hand at raising house plants. The specific needs of individual plants are covered in the following chapters. We have included photographs of plants as they have been used in homes and offices—as single plants; as groups in existing planters; as pieces of living, growing sculpture to add a note of warmth and a touch of softness. The lists of plants will give you many choices of plants whose growth requirements will suit your needs, in variety of leaf forms, colors, textures, shapes, and blooms.

WHERE TO OBTAIN HOUSE PLANTS

Most nurseries and garden shops have a special section containing house plants of all sizes and shapes. Supermarkets generally carry a few plants, and very often bargain shoppers can find some lovely plants. Florists specialize in many house plants and have a good assortment of flowering plants. For special or unusual plants, there are a number of mail order firms that will ship plants to you. Catalogs are available upon request that list available plants, their size and cost. People who grow plants indoors are a friendly and helpful group, and you may receive cuttings or leaves of plants from friends.

The containers, soil, fertilizer, and other items you might need can also be purchased at the places that sell the plants. Don't be afraid to ask questions and seek advice. Many a mistake can be avoided by doing so.

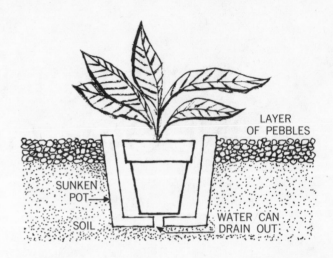

LARGE POTS sunk rim deep into indoor garden areas serve as containers for potted plants. A layer of pebbles makes a decorative covering and keeps mud from splashing up when the leaves are washed. Excess water drains through bottom of the large pot.

BIRD'S NEST FERN is brought in from lathhouse and set in a sunken pot. It will lift out easily.

DENDROBIUM ORCHIDS are brought in when in flower and can stay in place for several months.

GARDEN ROOM *adjoins bath. Room is radiant heated and kept near 70° so that tropical plants thrive here. Humidity is kept above normal by moist air from adjoining bath. Architect: Seth M. Fulcher.*

STAIRWAY *window is dramatic display area for large schefflera. Light comes from large window.*

TRAILING PHILODENDRON *decorates long divider wall. Plant receives light from nearby windows.*

HALLWAY *is made inviting by this arrangement. Large brass bowl contains grape ivy.*

LOBBY *of office building contains several large plants, including this* Ficus lyrata.

DECORATIVE *container complements schefflera. Pot in container is surrounded by sponge rock.*

SPACIOUS reception room is accented by a large planter. Contained in this one are several tree-sized scheffleras. Many other plants could be used as effectively.

DINING ROOM is handsomely complemented by six large hanging baskets containing grape ivy. The baskets are of wrought iron. Light comes in from narrow skylights and large windows on sides.

LOW CREDENZA becomes focal point of room by the use of schefflera in a colorful Mexican pot.

BAY WINDOW with south exposure is an ideal location for collection of plants. Awning controls light.

SPLIT-LEAF PHILODENDRON, bamboo in pots sunk in a permanent planter filled with vermiculite.

FIDDLELEAF FIG (Ficus lyrata) is happily situated on low bench facing a large north glass wall.

INTERESTING USE *of plants in a stairwell. Here you see dieffenbachia and podocarpus.*

AROUND SOFA *are* Cissus antarctica, Caryota, Chamaedorea elegans, *and dracaenas.*

SKYLIGHTED *garden provides perfect growing area. All rooms of the house open into it.*

TREE-SIZED SCHEFFLERA *responds to light and warmth by growing high and wide.*

PLANTS FOR FOLIAGE AND BLOSSOMS

They can add a new dimension to interior decor

There is technically no such thing as a house plant. The plants that have come to be known as house plants come from tropical areas and have become more or less adapted to the environment of the home, office, and commercial establishment. Therefore, the plants that are discussed in this book as plants to be used in the home are not necessarily most happy there. The native habitat of these plants should be kept in mind so that provisions can be made to meet their needs as much as possible.

By the same token, since there is no hard and fast rule as to what can be classed as a house plant, you may find plants that are not listed here that do well for you or that you have seen growing in someone's home. If there is a plant that pleases you, try it in your own home. Perhaps the plant can be an indoor-outdoor plant if it does not seem to adapt to a permanent life in the house. Try a plant in different areas of the house before deciding that it is not happy in the home environment—give it a chance to adjust.

GRAPE IVY and 'Hahn's Self-branching' ivy (corner) are placed on a wide shelf above a hallway in one of the Sunset *buildings. The ivies trail over the shelf in green cascades.*

LEAVES *of iron cross begonia are puckered, fuzzy. Colors are golden green marked with mahogany.*

DIEFFENBACHIAS *provide striking leaf variegations. These are* D. amoena, *native to Colombia.*

CHAMAEDOREA SEIFRIZII *is skylighted in an entrance hall. Upright form is ideal for narrow areas.*

DECORATIVE USES

In the previous chapter, many ideas were presented for the use of plants within the home or office. Some of these ideas may be adaptable for your own situation. Keep in mind that plants can be used in any room of the house.

If you want plants only for decorative purposes, choose them for their appearance and suitability to your setting. When they begin to look shabby, throw them away and replace them with new plants. If, on the other hand, you want plants not only for decoration but also for the pleasure and gratification that comes from growing them successfully, you must be willing to make a few adjustments in order to keep them healthy and attractive.

CONTAINERS

The standard clay pot is still the favorite container for house plants. It is available in a variety of shapes and sizes from the standard pot that is as tall as it is wide to the azalea or bulb pot that is much shallower. Plastic pots are available in all sizes and in a range of colors.

Pots and containers of the glazed variety are very attractive. Be certain to provide a drainage hole if the container does not have one. If that can't be accomplished, place a layer of pebbles in the bottom for drainage; do not overwater.

You may have a built-in planter or a portable one that can be used as a room divider or as a decorative accent in the living room or dining room. The most successful method of using a planter is to sink potted plants in sphagnum moss or peat in the planter. These pots can then be changed when the plants look straggly, turned if leaves face the light and not the direction best for being viewed, or changed when you have a blooming plant that you wish to display.

A container of your own design can be constructed of redwood. Be certain to provide some type of tray under such a box or planter (and under all potted plants) to keep water off the floor or rugs. Clay saucers will stain floor surfaces or rot rugs in time if the saucers are in direct contact with the surface. It is safer to use a glazed or metal saucer.

GROWTH CHARACTERISTICS

This chapter includes a wide variety of plants—from foliage plants that climb, trail, arch, or stand tall to all types of flowering plants. All sorts of growth habits are presented. The manner in which the plants grow is important to consider in relationship to the place in which you intend to locate your plants. A small apartment will not easily accommodate a tall

INTERNATIONAL collection of handsome containers: baskets, tubs, glazed and unglazed pots.

palm; conversely, a high-ceilinged room requires more than a small split-leaf philodendron.

GROWTH REQUIREMENTS

The following discussion covers the general culture of house plants. In the encyclopedia that follows, special or unusual requirements of individual plants are included.

Temperature: Since temperatures in the house are set for the comfort of human beings and not plants, there is not a great deal we can do to change them. There are, however, areas in the house that do vary in temperature a few degrees. For example, a window sill on a sunny day will have a higher reading than the interior of the room. If you live where the winters are very cold, protect plants in window areas by placing a shade, a drape, or newspapers between the plants and the glass, for that area will be colder than the room.

Variation in temperature can usually be provided by locating a plant either away from the heat source in a room or closer to it, according to the plant's requirements. If you have a plant that does not seem to be doing well in its present location, move it around until you find a spot where the plant prospers.

Light: Requirements for light vary with the individual plants. Most flowering plants require considerable light to bloom, while most foliage plants need diffused light. The only exception to this rule is plants that have variegated leaves. Leaf cells in the white spots contain little or no chlorophyll and hence are not capable of carrying on photosynthesis or food manufacturing. When a variegated plant is placed in a dark corner, the few green cells present in the leaves cannot manufacture enough carbohydrates to maintain a healthy growing condition.

Diffused light is that light which comes through a lightweight curtain placed over the window. A north window provides daylight but no direct sun. For plants that require full sun, a south window is best; sunlight comes in from this direction for the longest period during each day. Many plants will grow in the interior of homes or offices with no direct light. (See the chapter on Fluorescent Light Gardening, pages 84-89, for ideas on the use of artificial light in growing plants.)

Many gardeners move their house plants onto a shaded patio or terrace for the summer months. However, sudden temperature changes can be damaging; do not move house plants outside when there is much difference between the inside and the outside temperatures.

Water: Probably more failures in growing house plants result from incorrect watering than from any other factor. The roots of plants cannot breathe

HOLES can be drilled in some drainless pots. Brace inside of bottom with wood block, drill holes.

in soggy soil caused by overwatering. The opposite extreme is neglect in watering—plants will die if they do not receive water. When you do water, do it well, and then check daily to see if the plant is drying out. Push your finger down into the soil of the pot; the surface may feel dry, but the subsoil may still be moist. If the soil a half inch down in the pot is dry, it is time to water again. Water when the plant needs it, not according to a schedule. The temperature of the room, the relative humidity, the size of plant and its rate of growth, the size and type of container, and the potting mix are all factors which control the amount and frequency of need for water.

Use water that is warm or at room temperature. Most people use regular tap water, though there are those who feel that rain water is more beneficial. If your water goes through a water softener, do not use it on your plants. Obtain water from an outside faucet and allow it to warm to room temperature. Be certain that your potting soil drains well, and never allow plants to sit in a saucer of water.

Humidity: Here again the home and office are made to be comfortable for humans. The average relative humidity in the home or office is very low, especially when heating units are operating during the cold months. Many house plants require a higher humidity than is normally present. Use trays of pebbles in which water is placed to just below the tops of the pebbles. Place the pots on the pebbles, being certain that the bottoms are not sitting in the water. A daily syringing with a fine spray of water is also beneficial for the plants as it washes away the dust and raises the humidity slightly.

Fertilizing: There are many soluble house plant fertilizers on the market. These can be dissolved in water and easily applied. There are also some dry, slow release fertilizers on the market that are easy to use and effective. Follow the directions on the container carefully. Recent experience has indicated that more frequent application of fertilizer in a more dilute form is very beneficial. This provides nutrients in a steady supply instead of by fits and starts. You may find one method more beneficial for your plants than another. Experience will soon teach you what works best under your conditions.

Ventilation: All plants respond to ample ventilation. Fresh air is essential to plants just as it is to the human inhabitants of the room. Avoid cold drafts on the plants.

Pests, diseases, and control: A number of steps can be taken to prevent disease and infestations in plants. Keep your plants clean and well cared for. Wash leaves with a damp cloth at least once a month, especially those of large-leafed plants. There are commercially available leaf shine sprays if you wish a shine to the leaves. If the plants are not too large, a shower in the kitchen sink is beneficial. Keep all the faded flowers pinched off of flowering plants and remove all brown leaves. It is also beneficial to take plants outside once a month in spring and summer when the weather is mild. Place them in a shady place and hose off foliage. This is good for the plants and discourages infestation.

If there is evidence of insects, refer to the chapter on Pests and Diseases, pages 81-83. Spots on the leaves may be caused from too much sun or too much water. A general loss of leaves is probably due to overwatering. If the leaf color is not normal, overwatering is likely to be the cause. If there is a general yellowing of the lower leaves, underwatering is likely to be the cause. If the plant does not respond to treatment, it is best to discard it and replace it with another. Do not contaminate other plants with one that is infested.

POTTING AND REPOTTING

Some plants profit from being rootbound; others benefit from repotting every other year. (Check to see if roots are growing out of the drainage hole—if so it is time to repot.) In the year in between, remove some of the topsoil, add new soil, and cultivate lightly. This will remove some of the salts that have accumulated from watering and fertilizing.

The best time to repot plants is a matter of personal opinion. Some people like to repot in the summer so that the plants look nice by fall and winter when you need the color in the house. Others prefer spring as a time to repot.

In order to take the plant out of the pot, run a spatula or old table knife around the inside of the pot to loosen the root ball. Invert the pot, placing your hand over the root ball, and tap the pot gently on the edge of a table or bench. The plant and root ball should slide out easily. Unless the root ball is very dense and water has not been draining out of the pot well, it is unnecessary to disturb the root system. Move to a size larger pot with fresh soil placed at the base, sides, and top. Use clean pots, sterilized soil. Place a piece of broken pot (curved side facing upward) over the drainage hole before adding new soil. Leave space between top of soil and the top of the pot for water.

If you want to keep the plant in the same size pot, cut off a portion of the root ball on the bottom and each side, and then follow the directions above. To stimulate root growth the root ball may be scored in several places with a knife (make several ¼-inch cuts horizontally at intervals around root ball).

If the plant has not been growing well, remove soil carefully from the roots and then repot. As fresh soil is added tap the pot sharply on a solid surface to firm soil. Do not press the soil down from above as this might injure the roots.

After repotting, soak the plant by half-submerging the pot in a pail of water until soil is saturated; then allow plant to drain well. Do not water again until the soil is dry a half inch down from the soil surface.

BASIC MIX

3 CUBIC FEET

2 cubic feet	ground bark or other organic matter, nitrogen-treated
1 cubic foot	silty loam
¾ pound	dry complete fertilizer with 12 per cent nitrogen, half of it in readily available form (identified on label as *urea* after the nitrogen percentage)
2 pounds	limestone

ACID MIX

4 or 5 parts coarse-textured peat moss

    1 part composted oak leaf mold

Note: You can buy prepared mixes or use your own potting mix.

PROPAGATION

Spring and early summer is a good time to reshape or propagate house plants. After spending a winter indoors, plants may be leggy and in need of pinching and cutting back. From the pieces you cut off, you can easily grow new plants to replenish your supply or replace plants that have become too straggly and should be thrown away. Even the cuttings from such plants will be leggy, so often it is best to start with a new, stocky plant. Don't keep unsightly plants.

The only equipment you need is a box or pot filled with sand, sand and peat moss, perlite, or vermiculite. Cover the box or pot with a piece of glass or plastic or a plastic bag. There are a number of ways to propagate house plants: by seed or seedlings, leaf cuttings, stem cuttings, layering, and dividing. All of these procedures must be carried out indoors.

Leaf cuttings: Probably the easiest method of increasing indoor foliage plants is by leaf cuttings. African violet, peperomia, and sansevieria, for example, can be propagated this way.

The leaf—or, in the case of sansevieria, a portion of it—will root easily in clean, sharp river sand. Firm the cuttings in the rooting medium, and keep the medium moist but not wet until cuttings are rooted and ready to transplant into the potting medium.

The leaves of Rex begonias and other fibrous-rooted begonias will produce plants from their primary veins. Insert leaves in rooting medium or pin to the surface.

Softwood cuttings: Philodendron, ivy, and croton, to name a few, are readily propagated from softwood cuttings. Cut a 2 to 3-inch length of stem with two or three leaves attached. With a sharp knife, cut the stem from the parent plant just below a leaf node. Remove foliage from the portion which will be below the surface of the rooting medium. Dip the cut end into hormone powder to hasten rooting. Then plant the cuttings, firm the medium, and water thoroughly to establish contact between the cutting and the rooting medium. Roots will develop at the base of the cutting and around the leaf nodes or joints.

Cuttings of geraniums, impatiens, coleus, ivy, and philodendrons can be rooted in water and then planted.

Stem cuttings: Many philodendrons, dracaena, and dieffenbachia can be propagated by cutting a portion of the heavy, canelike stem. Cut sections with two or three joints. Wrap this type of cutting with moist sphagnum moss. New shoots will be produced from the eyes.

Layering: This is a method of propagation frequently used on many of the philodendrons and ivies with vining growth habits. Bend the stems over the edge of the pot and lay them in a horizontal position on the rooting medium. After roots have formed, cut

1. REMOVE cuttings, 1 to 2-inch growth tips, from geraniums with a new razor blade.

2. STRIP leaves from lower halves of cuttings, remove all blossoms or buds before placing in pots.

3. FIRM cuttings into moist perlite in clay pot. Most varieties will root within a week or two.

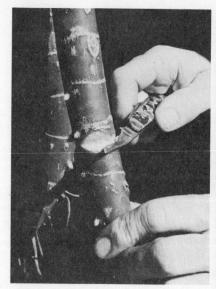

AIR LAYERING: Brace stem and cut ½ to ⅔ through. Place moist sphagnum moss in cut, wrap more around stem, cover with plastic, tie. When roots form, remove and plant rooted portion.

the stem in sections. The roots and shoot formed at each node will be the start of a new plant.

The same technique can be used for plants that produce new plants on runners. The new plant can be placed on the rooting medium and the runner cut when roots have formed.

Air layering: This is a very old but nevertheless a very satisfactory technique. It is especially useful in the propagation of plants that are difficult to grow from cuttings and for tall, lank, one-stemmed plants that cannot be bent to the ground for tip layering or which offer no side shoots for cutting material.

The principle behind this method is really quite simple. The stem is cut, girdled, or scarified to stimulate root formation. When the roots have formed, they are cut off together with the stem and leaves above and become a separate plant.

First cut into the stem below a node, cutting half to two thirds of the way through the stem. Then place some moist sphagnum moss in the cut and a couple of handfuls around the stem. Wrap with plastic film and tie in place at the top and bottom. When roots show through the plastic, sever rooted portion from parent plant and pot. New growth will be stimulated from the parent plant, and you will also have a new plant.

Division: Plants that form multiple crowns can most easily be increased by dividing them. For example, *Spathiphylum*, sansevieria, and Chinese evergreen have this type of growth habit and can be divided easily.

Seed: Often plants that cannot be obtained in any other form can be purchased as seeds. Growing plants from seeds can be enjoyable and is an inexpensive way to increase your plant collection. Follow directions on the seed packet carefully.

ENCYCLOPEDIA

A wide range of foliage and flowering plants is encompassed by the following list of plants. Many of them are old favorites, while others are new. The culture of plants in general has preceded this list. However, if any plant requires special treatment, it is explained here.

Adiantum raddianum (A. cuneatum, maidenhair fern): Fronds cut 3 or 4 times. Many varieties with differing textures and compactness. Plant benefits by being moved to sheltered, shaded patio in summer.

Aglaonema: Ornamental foliage. Flowers resemble small green callas. Does well in poor light; requires frequent watering.

A. commutatum: Grows to 2 feet. Dark green leaves marked with veins of pale green. Flowers are followed by clusters of yellow to red berries.

A. modestum (Chinese evergreen): Easily grown plant 2-3 feet in height. Leaves shiny dark green to 18 inches long, 5 inches across.

Aluminum plant: See *Pilea cadierei*

Amaryllis: See *Hippeastrum*

Anthurium: Lustrous flower bracts of red, pink, or white. Leaves are dark green. This plant requires high humidity—over 50 per cent. High temperatures are best (80°-90°), but the plant will grow at house temperatures. Needs strong light, but not direct sun. Mix for potting should be coarse, porous.

Aphelandra squarrosa: Large, 8 to 12-inch-long, dark green leaves veined with white. Colorful spikes are formed at the tips of the stems by yellow flowers, tipped with green. To make plants bushy, cut stems back to one or two pairs of leaves after flowering. Give the plant morning sun. May be moved to patio in mild weather if placed in protected area. Variety 'Louisae' is best known, but newer varieties are more compact and leaves show more variation.

Artillery plant: See *Pilea microphylla*

Asparagus falcatus (sickle-thorn asparagus): Excellent foliage mass. Leaves 2-3 inches long in clusters of 3-5 at ends of branches. Tiny, white, fragrant flowers in loose clusters followed by brown berries. Will survive much neglect. Tolerates poor light. Cut back if plant becomes too large.

A. sprengeri: Arching, drooping stems 3-6 feet long with bright green needle-like leaves 1 inch long. Pinkish flowers in loose clusters. Good in hanging baskets. Can go indoors and outdoors.

Aspidistra elatior (cast-iron plant): Sturdy foliage plant. Leaf blades 1-2½ feet long, 3-4 inches wide, tough, glossy, and dark green. Extremely tolerant; requires minimum care. Responds to feeding in spring and summer. The variegated form 'Variegata' has leaves striped with white.

Asplenium nidus (bird's nest fern): Striking foliage plant with upright fronds 4 feet long. Plant benefits by being moved to shady patio in the summer.

Aucuba japonica 'Crotonifolia': Leaves heavily splashed with white and gold. Shrub clothed with polished leaves, edges toothed. Use to light up dark corners. Also can be moved out onto a shady patio in the summer.

A. 'Variegata': Dark green leaves spotted with yellow. This is the most familiar aucuba.

Balsam: See *Impatiens*

Begonia: Remarkable for rich colors, varied leaf textures and patterns, forms of flowers and foliage. Stems and leaves may be hairy or smooth. Growth habit erect to trailing. Rex begonias have spectacularly colored and patterned leaves. Best in filtered shade in rich, porous, slightly acid soil with good drainage and ample moisture.

Bird's nest fern: See *Asplenium nidus*

Boston fern: See *Nephrolepis exaltata* 'Bostoniense'

Brassaia actinophylla (Schefflera, umbrella tree): Usually sold as schefflera. Desirable foliage plant. Horizontal tiers of long-stalked leaves are divided into 7-16 large leaflets radiating outward like the ribs of an umbrella (hence the common name). Cut tips occasionally to keep plant from becoming leggy. Keep in part shade or deep shade. Water heavily and feed frequently for fast growth.

Busy Lizzy: See *Impatiens*

Caladium bicolor: Showy leaves are large, arrow-shaped, long-stalked, colored in bands and blotches of red, rose, pink, white, silver, bronze, and green.

Start tubers in March. Pot in a mix of equal parts coarse sand, leaf mold, and ground bark or peat moss. Use 5-inch pot for 2½-inch tuber, 7-inch pot for one larger or two smaller tubers. Fill pot halfway with mix; stir in heaping teaspoon of fish meal. Add 1 inch of mix; set tuber with knobby side up, cover with 2 inches of mix, and water thoroughly. Keep soil moist, not wet. As leaves develop, water more frequently. Gradually withhold water when the leaves start to die down. In about a month, lift tubers, remove most of soil, dry for 10 days. Store for winter in dry peat moss or vermiculite at temperatures between 50° and 60°.

REX BEGONIAS are available in a wide range of colors; keep them out of direct sun, and water well.

CALADIUMS have varicolored leaves and are strikingly veined. Keep warm, moist, away from sun.

CLIVIAS *are deep orange in color and bloom in the spring. They make colorful house plants.*

CROCUS *can be forced into bloom for early spring color. Here they are placed in an ice cream carton lid.*

Cast-iron plant: See *Aspidistra elatior*

Chamaedorea costaricana: Bamboo-like clumps of 8-10 trunks if well watered and fed. Lacy, feathery leaves. Will eventually need large container.

C. elegans (parlor palm): Widely sold as *Neanthe bella.* Best indoor chamaedorea. Tolerates crowded roots and poor light. Single stem grows slowly to 3-4 feet. Douse with water occasionally; feed regularly. Repot every 2-3 years, carefully washing off old soil and replacing with good potting mix. Effective planted 2 or 3 to a container.

C. erumpens: Slow growing, cluster-forming, bamboo-like dwarf with drooping leaves. Needs shade.

C. geonomaeformis: Broad, oblong leaves deeply split at tips to give fishtail effect. Grows slowly to 4 feet.

Chamaeranthemum: Foliage in different colors with vein patterns. Some have small flowers. Needs high humidity and diffused sunlight. Keep well watered but not soggy.

Chinese evergreen: See *Aglaonema modestum*

Chlorophytum comosum: Clumps of grasslike blades, some with white-margined leaves. Miniature duplicates of mother plant produced at ends of curved stems. Offsets can be cut off and potted individually. Grow in fully lighted window.

Cissus antarctica (kangaroo treebine): Vine climbing by tendrils. Medium green, shiny leaves, 2-3½ inches long and as wide, with toothed edges. Grows in part shade or shade; can go outside in the summer. Will tumble down or climb.

C. rhombifolia (grape ivy): Lovely dark green foliage. Leaves divided into diamond-shaped leaflets 1-4 inches long with sharp-toothed edges. Has bronze overtones because of reddish hairs on veins beneath. Tolerates low light intensities well.

Clivia miniata (Kaffir lily): Member of amaryllis family. Brilliant clusters of orange, funnel-shaped flowers rise from dense clumps of green, strap-shaped leaves. Blooms December to April. Red berries follow flowers. Grow in ample light—no direct sun—in rich, moist soil. Plant with tops of fleshy roots just below soil line. Fertilize 2 or 3 times during growing season.

Codiaeum variegatum (croton): Large, leathery, glossy leaves which may be green, yellow, red, purple, bronze, pink, or any combination of these. Leaves may be oval, lance-shaped, or narrow, straight-edged or lobed. Usually single-stemmed, 6-24 inches tall. Grows best in warm, humid, well lighted place.

Coffea arabica: Shining, dark green, oval leaves to 6 inches long. Small fragrant flowers followed by red ½-inch fruits. Each contains two seeds—coffee beans. Grow in well lighted room; can go out on a shady patio in the summer.

Coleus blumei: Brilliantly colored leaves in shades of green, chartreuse, yellow, buff, salmon, peach, orange, red, magenta, purple, and brown, often with several colors to a leaf. Leaves are oval, 3-6 inches long, with scalloped, toothed, or fringed margins. Grows best in strong, indirect light or thin shade. Needs warmth, ample water, and fertilizer. Pinch back to encourage branching. Remove flower buds.

Crocus: For early spring color indoors, crocus can be forced. Plant corms in pots in the fall. Showy, colorful cups appear above grasslike foliage. Needs sun. (See *Narcissus* for techniques.)

Croton: See *Codiaeum variegatum*

Cyclamen (florists'): Blooms from late fall to early spring; flowers resemble shooting stars. Plant seedlings in September in rich, porous mix, or buy potted plants in bloom. When planting a tuber place upper half of tuber above soil level. Keep soil moist and place plants so they receive early or late sun.

Daffodil: See *Narcissus*

Dieffenbachia amoena: Striking variegated leaves 18 inches long marked with narrow, slanting white stripes. Grows to 6 feet or higher. Give ample north light, turn occasionally, and water when dry. Air layer leggy plants. Feed bimonthly.

D. 'Exotica': Smaller than other dieffenbachias. Leaves dull green with creamy white variegations.

D. picta: Wide, oval, green leaves 10 inches or more in length with greenish white dots and patches. The variety 'Rudolph Roehrs' is widely sold. *D. p.* 'Superba' has thicker foliage, more creamy white dots and splotches.

Dizygotheca elegantissima (threadleaf false aralia): Leaves on juvenile plant lacy—divided fanwise into very narrow, 4 to 9-inch-long leaflets with notched edges, dark shiny green above, reddish beneath. More mature plants have longer leaves. Give ample light but not direct sunshine. Grow in fast-draining soil. Feed monthly.

Dracaena deremensis 'Warneckii': Small, palm-like plants. Leaves are 2 feet long, 2 inches wide, rich green, striped white and gray. Slow-growing to 15 feet tall.

D. fragrans 'Massangeana': Heavy, ribbon-like, blue-green leaves to 3 feet long, 4 inches wide. (Typical plant in an 8-inch pot will bear leaves about 18 inches long.) Has broad yellow stripe in center of leaf. Tolerates a darker location in the house than will other dracaenas.

D. godseffiana: Smaller than other dracaenas. Slender erect or spreading stems with pairs or trios of 5-inch-long, 2-inch-wide leaves. Dark green spotted in white.

D. marginata: Clusters of blade-shaped, deep olive green leaves edged with red.

COLEUS is a colorful foliage plant for indoors. This one is spotlighted by lamp; basket has metal liner.

MULTIPLE-STEMMED palm, variegated dracaena on pebble-filled tray which catches excess water.

HYACINTH blooming in a special glass. Roots are visible below while the fragrant flower rises above.

D. sanderiana: Neat and upright, resembling a young corn plant. Strap-shaped, 9-inch-long leaves striped white.

English ivy: See *Hedera helix*

Evergreen grape: See *Rhoicissus capensis*

Fatsia japonica (Japanese aralia): Good for cool, bright room with north or east exposure. Big, glossy, dark green, deeply lobed, fanlike leaves on long stalks. Remove flowers for bigger leaves.

Ficus benjamina (weeping Chinese banyan): Shiny green, leathery, poplar-like leaves on drooping branches. Can be placed outside in the summer.

F. diversifolia: Twisted, open branch pattern. Thick, roundish, dark green 2-inch leaves with tan specks. Small fruits (actually tiny figs) borne continuously. Place in strong diffused light, part shade outside on a deck or patio.

F. elastica 'Decora' (rubber plant): One of the most foolproof indoor plants. Leaves are thick, glossy, leathery dark green, 8-12 inches long by 4-6 inches wide. New leaves are bronzy color.

F. lyrata (fiddleleaf fig): Dramatic structural form with huge, dark green, fiddle-shaped leaves to 15 inches long and 10 inches wide. To increase branching, pinch back when young.

Fiddleleaf fig: See *Ficus lyrata*

Fittonia verschaffeltii: Leaves dark green, oval, 4 inches long, conspicuously veined with red. Low and creeping. North light with high humidity is desirable. Can be grown from cuttings. Good in terrariums.

F. v. 'Argyroneura': Vivid green, papery oval leaves veined with white.

Freckle face: See *Hypoestes sanguinolenta*

Geranium: See *Pelargonium*

Grape ivy: See *Cissus rhombifolia*

Gynura aurantiaca (velvet plant): Fleshy leaves with violet or purple hairs which give a velvety texture. Grow in a bright light or full sun. Water to keep evenly moist but not soggy.

Hedera helix (English ivy): Leaves dark, dull green, lobed, 2-4 inches wide and as long. Good as ground cover under taller house plants. Several good small-leafed varieties.

Hippeastrum (amaryllis): Bulb. From two to several flowers, often 8-9 inches across, form on stout 2-foot stems. Colors include reds, pinks, white, salmon, near orange, some variously marked and striped. Blooms in spring. The broad, strap-shaped leaves usually appear after flowers, grow through summer, disappear in fall.

Pot the bulbs in rich, sandy soil mix with the addition of bonemeal. Plant between November and February. Allow 2-inch space between bulb and edge of pot. Set upper half of bulb above soil surface, firm soil, and water well. Keep barely moist until growth starts.

To force early bloom, keep plant in a warm, dark place until it has rooted. When flower stalk is 6 inches high, place in sunny window. Increase watering as leaves form; feed lightly every 2 weeks through flowering period. When flowers fade, cut off stem; continue watering; feed to encourage leaf growth. When leaves yellow, withhold water, let plants dry out. Repot in late fall or early winter.

Howeia belmoreana (sentry palm): Over-arching leaves, slightly more compact than *H. forsteriana*. This is the kentia palm of the florists. Stands some watering neglect, drafts, and dust.

H. forsteriana: Larger than *H. belmoreana*. Leaves to 9 feet with long, drooping leaflets.

Hoya carnosa (wax flower or wax plant): Vining plant with 2 to 4-inch-long oval leaves. Round, tight clusters of creamy white flowers—tiny 5-pointed pink star in the center of each. Fragrant, summer blooming. Water deeply in summer, then allow soil to go dry and water again. Grow in a sunny window.

Hyacinthus: Bulb. Bell-shaped, fragrant flowers on spikes that rise from basal leaves. Colors are white and cream through shades of pink, red, purple, and blue. The bulbs can be grown in water in a special hyacinth glass (see photograph on this page) or are suitable for pot culture (see *Narcissus* for potting instructions).

Hypoestes sanguinolenta (freckle face): Oval leaves spotted with pink. Attractive plant with slender stems. Pinch tips to induce bushiness.

Impatiens (balsam, busy Lizzy, touch-me-not): Showy flowers in many colors. Plant several to a pot. Needs lots of water. There are dwarf varieties.

Japanese aralia: See *Fatsia japonica*

Jerusalem cherry: See *Solanum pseudo-capsicum*

Kaffir lily: See *Clivia miniata*

Kangaroo treebine: See *Cissus antarctica*

Kentia palm: See *Howeia belmoreana*

Maidenhair fern: See *Adiantum raddianum*

Maranta leuconeura (prayer plant): Leaves 7-8 inches long, whitish along midrib and veins with brown spots toward margin—spots look like rabbit tracks (another common name for this plant). Leaves fold upward at night. Grows in north light. Must have warmth, occasional trimming, and regular feeding. Excellent in dish gardens, terrariums, or shallow pots.

M. l. massangeana: Low plant with striking leaves. Blue-green leaves have silver midrib and pink lines radiating out to margin. Undersides of leaves are red-purple.

Monstera deliciosa (split-leaf philodendron): Vine with leathery, dark green leaves, deeply cut and perforated with holes. Long, cordlike roots hanging from stems root into soil or moss "totem poles." Feed occasionally; keep leaves clean. In poor light or low humidity leaves will be smaller. When plant is bare at bottom and in good condition, transfer to larger pot and plant younger, lower plant at base.

Moses-in-the-cradle: See *Rhoeo spathacea*

Narcissus (daffodil): Bulb. Flowers with a ring of segments at right angles to the trumpet—single on a stem or clustered. Colors basically yellow and white, but with many variations.

Plant large-sized bulbs in fall for winter blooms. Use porous mix of equal parts loam, coarse sand, and peat moss, ground bark, or leaf mold. Set bulbs in pots so that the tips are level with the soil surface. Water thoroughly. Place pots in a cool, dark place and cover with peat moss, sawdust, or inverted flats. After 8-12 weeks check to see if roots are coming through the drainage hole in the bottom. When roots are visible, move pots to a light spot. When the tops are green, move to sun. Keep well watered until foliage yellows; fertilize 2 or 3 times after leaves form. Bulbs that are forced seldom do well the second year. They can be planted in the garden.

Neanthe bella: See *Chamaedorea elegans*

Nephrolepis exaltata 'Bostoniense' (Boston fern): Spreading, arching habit with graceful, drooping fronds. Grow in north light in a cool room. Feed each month with dilute fertilizer; water whenever soil becomes dry.

Nephthytis: See *Syngonium podophyllum*

Panamiga: See *Pilea involucrata*

Pandanus veitchii (screwpine): Long, narrowing leaves form a rosette. Leaves are margined with white, small spines. Compact form available. Tolerates reduced light, warm conditions. Water by drenching soil and letting dry out before watering again.

Parlor palm: See *Chamaedorea elegans*

Pelargonium (geranium): Many kinds—different flower and leaf forms, some scented. Need to be somewhat potbound to bloom best. When repotting, move to the next size larger. Water frequently in warm weather. Keep removing faded flowers to encourage new bloom. Pinch growing tips in early stages of growth. Prune late in fall. Place in sunny window or brightest light possible.

SPLIT-LEAF PHILODENDRON growing in 6-inch pot is 2 feet tall. Longest leaf is 14 inches.

PEPEROMIAS *for dish gardens, some to trail, others upright. Chopsticks are for tamping soil.*

MORE PEPEROMIAS: *top to bottom,* P. 'Astrid', P. griseoargentea, *and* P. obtusifolia 'Lougenii'.

PHILODENDRON REGELIANUM *has a simple, bold form. Here it complements a Chinese painting.*

LEAVES *of climbing Philodendron 'Hastatum Rubrum' have maroon cast, red undersides, stems.*

Peperomia: Often succulent, usually prostrate or trailing. Use in planters, dish gardens, or other containers. Can be used as ground cover in large indoor planting. Grow in north light or diffused light protected from sun, in cool or warm temperature.

Philodendron: Many kinds with many different leaf shapes and sizes. Vining types must be tied until they shape themselves, even though they climb. Support can be anything, but water absorbent columns (tree fern, slabs of redwood bark, wire and sphagnum "totem poles") serve well because they can be kept moist, and the moist column helps the plants grow better. Self-heading types form short, broad plants with leaves radiating out from a central point.

Grow in good light but not direct sun. Give ample water, but avoid soggy soil. Feed lightly. Dust leaves once a month. As lower leaves drop (as they will on older plants), air layer leafy top part and replant. Or cut plant back to short stub and allow to start over. Aerial roots may be pushed into the soil or pole or cut off.

Phoenix roebelenii (pigmy date palm): Fine-leafed, small-scale palm. One stem grows slowly to 6 feet or so. Curved leaves form dense crown. Not successful for dark corners; keep moist.

Piggy-back plant: See *Tolmiea menziesii*

Pigmy date palm: See *Phoenix roebelenii*

Pilea cadierei (aluminum plant): Juicy-stemmed foliage plant growing to 1-1½ feet tall. Fast-growing. Leaves small, fleshy, toothed, vivid green to bluish green with conspicuous silver blotches. Tiny flowers. Grow in light shade or bright light. Water thoroughly; don't water again until soil surface feels dry. Feed monthly.

P. involucrata (panamiga): Freely branching plant 6-8 inches tall. Roundish small leaves, brownish green above, purplish beneath, heavily veined in a seersucker effect.

P. microphylla (artillery plant): Many spreading branches and fine twigs. Tiny bright green leaves are set close together on the branches; total effect is somewhat fernlike.

Plectranthus oertendahlii: Thick leaves marked with silver veins and edged with purplish scalloped margins. Small white flowers are carried on spikes. Good for trailing over shelf edge or in a hanging container.

Pothos: See *Rhapidophora aurea*

Prayer plant: See *Maranta leuconeura*

Rhaphidophora aurea (pothos): Related and similar to philodendron. Treat same as climbing philodendrons. Oval, leathery leaves 2-4 inches long, bright green, splashed with yellow. Best as trailer in dish gardens, planting boxes, and pots on shelves and mantels.

PHILODENDRON OXYCARDIUM is adaptable to the warm, dry atmosphere of most living rooms.

Rhoeo spathacea (Moses-in-the-cradle): Sword-shaped dark green leaves (deep purple beneath) carried in tufts of a dozen or so on 8-inch-long stems. Flowers, small and white, crowded into boat-shaped bracts down among the leaves. Good in hanging basket. Will take high or low light intensity and casual watering.

Rhoicissus capensis (evergreen grape): Leaves roundish to kidney-shaped, scallop-toothed, something like true grape. New growth rosy rust with red hairs beneath. Will take heavy shade; needs to be moist.

Ruellia makoyana: Low-growing plant with green leaves shaded violet and silvery veins. Requires high humidity—good for terrariums. Place in filtered or diffused sunlight. Potting soil should be kept moist.

LARGE, high-ceilinged garden room provides ample light for growing a variety of plants.

Rubber plant: See *Ficus elastica* 'Decora'

Sansevieria (snake plant): Thick, patterned leaves grow in a cluster and radiate out from base. Leaves vary from short, blunt triangles to long swords. Water infrequently but thoroughly. Will grow in much or little light, seldom needs repotting, and will withstand considerable neglect.

Saxifraga stolonifera (strawberry geranium): Creeping plant that makes runners like those of strawberry plant. Nearly round, white-veined leaves, pink underneath. Flowers white in loose clusters. Can be planted in hanging baskets. Keep moist.

Schefflera: See *Brassaia actinophylla*

Screwpine: See *Pandanus veitchii*

Sentry palm: See *Howeia belmoreana*

Sickle-thorn asparagus: See *Asparagus falcatus*

Snake plant: See *Sansevieria*

Solanum pseudo-capsicum (Jerusalem cherry): Deep green leaves. Showy scarlet fruits like miniature tomatoes in October-December. Fruits may be poisonous to eat. Many dwarf strains.

Spathiphyllum: Dark green leaves are large and oval or elliptical and narrowed to a point. Leaf stalks rise directly from soil. Flowers resemble calla lilies or anthuriums—a central column of closely set tiny flowers surrounded by a leaflike white flower bract. Grow in good light but not hot, sunny windows. Feed weekly with liquid fertilizer. Grows and blooms readily indoors.

Split-leaf philodendron: See *Monstera deliciosa*

Sprekelia formosissima: Spidery, orchid-like, dark crimson blossoms. Stems are 12 inches tall, and foliage resembles that of daffodils. Grow in pots the same as amaryllis, only slightly cooler. Repot every 3 or 4 years.

Strawberry geranium: See *Saxifraga stolonifera*

Syngonium podophyllum (Nephthytis): Related to philodendron. Long-stalked, arrow-shaped, dull green, sometimes lobed and variegated. Useful in terrariums and dish gardens, as a trailer, or trained against a support.

Threadleaf false aralia: See *Dizygotheca elegantissima*

Tolmiea menziesii (piggy-back plant): Abundant production of attractive, 5-inch-wide basal leaves—shallowly lobed and toothed, rather hairy. Leaves can produce new plantlets at the junction of leafstalk and blade. Inconspicuous greenish brown flowers. Tolerates wet soil.

Touch-me-not: See *Impatiens*

Tradescantia fluminensis (wandering Jew): Easy-to-grow plant of prostrate or trailing habit. Dark green oval or oblong leaves attached to succulent stem at the swollen joints. Tiny flowers are not showy. Excellent for dish gardens. ('Variegata' has leaves striped with yellow or white.)

Tulipa: Some dainty and whimsical, others tall and stately. (See *Narcissus* for culture.) Plant in October for spring display. Many colors available.

Umbrella tree: See *Brassaia actinophylla*

Velvet plant: See *Gynura aurantiaca*

Wandering Jew: See *Tradescantia fluminensis* and *Zebrina pendula*

Wax flower: See *Hoya carnosa*

Wax plant: See *Hoya carnosa*

Weeping Chinese banyan: See *Ficus benjamina*

Zebrina pendula (wandering Jew): Same growth habit and leaf shape as *Tradescantia fluminensis*, but not as large. Variegated form Z. *pendula* 'Quadricolor' has purplish green leaves with bands of white, pink, and red.

TRY *herbs in 6-inch pots placed in lettuce baskets. Pottery saucers catch the drips.*

PEPEROMIA *cuttings provide greens for this simple arrangement. The cuttings will root in the water.*

SPATHIPHYLLUM *needs warmth, ample water and humidity. Room temperature should be 60° or above.*

PHILODENDRON SELLOUM *is planted in a 10-inch pot. Largest leaf is 2 feet long, 18 inches wide.*

FERNS, *in various shades. Left to right: Asparagus falcatus, English hedge fern, bird's nest fern.*

FRONDS *of squirrel's foot fern cover hanging basket. Lift fronds to see furry "feet."*

TROPICAL *foliage plants tempt shoppers in supermarkets. Many are rooted cuttings that can be transplanted into larger pots. Bargains can often be found.*

A good indoor project for a winter day is planting a bottle garden. Once completed it will take care of itself and will not even require watering if the bottle's opening is small. Some gardens have been known to continue growing for a period of several years, although they tend to get a bit overgrown over the years.

Choosing a container. The bottle you choose can be anything from a quart salad oil bottle to a 5-gallon carboy or an antique liquor bottle. Be sure it is clean and dry and has a neck wide enough to push a small plant through. Clear or lightly tinted glass bottles show off plants to their best advantage.

Choosing the plants. Select plants that can withstand moist soil, high humidity, and low light intensity. Choose slow-growing types in scale with the container you plan to use. Don't worry about using small plants—under optimum growing conditions even the slow-growing types will fill in fast. For this same reason, don't try to crowd too many plants into one container. One small vine forming a tracery up the side of a slender bottle can be most effective.

Here are some adaptable plants:

Ground covers. Moss, selaginella, wandering Jew *(Zebrina pendula)*.

Medium-height plants. Acorus, ardisia, Chinese evergreen *(Aglaonema modestum)*, dracaena, fittonia, maranta, pilea, small-leafed ivies.

Taller plants. Croton, umbrella plant *(Cyperus alternifolius)*, many ferns (holly, asparagus), screw pine *(Pandanus)*, pigmy date palm, small-leafed philodendron.

Preparation for Planting

Soil. A basic potting mix containing equal parts coarse river sand, garden loam, and leaf mold is a good one for a bottle garden. To two quarts of this mix add a half cup each of fine charcoal and perlite. Water down the mix with a mild liquid fertilizer, then sterilize it in a 300° oven for 30 minutes.

Or use a sterilized package mix, available at nurseries and garden centers for use in planters; but avoid a rich soil mix, or plants may become lanky.

Drainage. Because there is no way for water to drain out of the bottle, place a 1-inch layer of charcoal or crushed rock on the bottom for drainage. Cover this with 2-3 inches of soil mix.

Tools for planting. Make a slender funnel, long enough to reach nearly to the bottom of the bottle, from a sheet of stiff paper. Pour drainage material and soil through it to keep sides of the bottle clean. A length of flexible copper tubing, a pronged wooden stick, or a 12-inch-long glass pipette makes a good tool for planting. Work a piece of rubber tubing onto the end of the pipette to provide a flexible tip that won't damage plant roots.

Planting

Carefully wash all soil from the roots of the plants, inspecting each plant to make sure it is healthy and free of insects. Make a hole for the plant's roots in the soil mix, then carefully ease the plant—roots first—down through the neck of the bottle and into the hole, using tweezers. Use the rod or stick to tamp the soil down around the roots.

To work out the best arrangement, set the tallest plants in place first and work in the ground covers last. If you use a soil just moist enough to hold together when pressed in the palm of the hand, you will not have to water the plants after they are set in place. Use a cotton swab to wipe off dirt that may have clung to the glass sides.

Care of a Bottle Garden

Keep bottle gardens in good light but out of the sun's direct rays, which can burn them quickly. Thin out rapidly growing plants when foliage gets too dense. You have bottled up the climate along with the plants, and this is one part of your indoor garden that will take care of itself indefinitely.

AFRICAN VIOLETS

These universal favorites are versatile, easy for beginners

It is difficult to find any other house plant that has as much to offer as the African violet. Its foliage is attractive; it produces flowers almost all year; and it is available in a variety of sizes, tailor-made to fit any space.

Growing African violets doesn't require constant fussing, and you don't need great skill or long experience to be successful at it. With a reasonable amount of care, the plants will thrive as well for the beginner as for an expert.

STAGE or platform is excellent for the display of a collection of African violets. The tray is filled with pebbles, and water is added. This provides additional humidity for the plants.

'LILIAN JARRETT' has dark green foliage streaked with light green. The flowers are double, soft pink.

'NORSEMAN' is an old favorite. It has dark green foliage and single flowers of clear blue.

TRAILING SPECIES of African violets are ideal for hanging baskets. Hang one in kitchen window.

'DOLLY DIMPLE' is a miniature that fits into a teacup. It has light blue flowers, girl foliage.

'CAMBRIDGE PINK', double-flowered, with center of deeper pink, has won many blue ribbons.

'WEDGEWOOD' has medium-blue double flowers, bronzy leaves. Plant may grow to 30 inches across.

DECORATIVE USES FOR AFRICAN VIOLETS

These lovely plants have long been windowsill favorites and look very attractive there. They also are very attractive displayed as a group on a low table, plant stand, or planter. Artificial light has proved very useful for growing these plants and can provide a means for growing them on a dark book shelf or other dimly lighted area. A large brandy snifter or round glass bowl makes an attractive home for a single African violet. Surround the pot with sphagnum moss inside the bowl, and then the pot can be exchanged for another when blooming is finished.

CONTAINERS

Either clay (glazed or unglazed) or plastic pots can be used for African violets. If plastic or glazed pots are used, be certain to avoid overwatering. Violets need to be moist, but the soil should never be soggy.

When using unglazed pots, make a collar of aluminum foil around the edge of the pot. This will prevent burning of the leaf stalks. (Unglazed pots absorb and accumulate harmful salts.)

GROWTH REQUIREMENTS

If you have never grown African violets, a few guides to their general culture will be helpful. Soon you will develop methods of care that you will find more beneficial for your plants in the environment in which you grow them.

Temperature: A constant room temperature of 65°-75° is best for these plants; they may lose blooms if temperature varies more than 12°. During months when the furnace is in use, provide additional humidity by setting small bowls of water near the plants, or place the plants in shallow trays filled with small pebbles and water. The pots should not sit in water, so keep the level just below that of the tops of the stones. For most effective display, group plants together rather than scattering them.

Light: African violets need 12-15 hours of diffused light daily; direct sunlight will burn foliage. If you aren't able to provide adequate natural light, you can supplement daylight with table lamps or fluorescent lights (see chapter on Fluorescent Light Gardening on pages 84-89).

Water: More African violet troubles are caused by overwatering than by underwatering. Water only when the surface of the soil feels dry. You'll find that glazed or plastic pots hold moisture longer than clay pots do.

Fertilizing: It's best for the beginner to use a liquid or dry commercial plant food made especially for

ASSORTMENT of violet leaves: 1, plain boy; 2, girl; 3, oak leaf; 4, quilted; 5, fluted; 6, serrated; 7, variegated; 8, black-green; 9, rippled; 10, elongated wavy. Flowers: A, plain single; B, semi-double; C, single star; D, double 'Supreme'; E, single fringed; F, variegated double; G, fringed double; H, crested double; I, fantasy. Scale: Each square is 1 inch.

African violets. After you've become experienced with your plants, you may want to try different kinds of fertilizer. Some specialists start feeding their plants a weak solution of a water soluble fertilizer (¼ teaspoon to 2 quarts water) as soon as they show new growth; others wait until plants have finished their first blooming period. Whichever method you use, don't fertilize more often than every two weeks —and never when the soil is dry. (Water at least 2 hours before you apply any fertilizer.)

Two other jobs requiring regular attention might be worked in with the fertilizing schedule so you don't overlook them. First of the month, fertilize; second of the month, remove suckers with a nut pick or sharp tweezers; third of the month, spray for pests and diseases. A number of aerosol sprays on the market are effective for controlling pests on African violets. When using either sprays or fertilizer, be sure to follow the manufacturer's directions.

POTTING AND REPOTTING

When plants are large enough to repot, plant each in a separate pot—either clay or plastic. For your first experiments with African violets, it's easiest to use new pots; old ones must be sterilized. To save yourself the inconvenience of sterilizing soil, use one of the excellent African violet mixes available in garden shops or nurseries.

PROPAGATION

Most African violet specialists like to propagate their plants from leaf cuttings. They are usually delighted to talk with anyone interested in their plants and are quite willing to share a few leaves. In addition, you can buy plants at a florist's or nursery, or you can order leaves or plants started as leaf cuttings from African violet growers who handle mail orders.

You can root leaf cuttings in water or plant them directly in a rooting medium. If you have several leaves, you may want to try both methods to see which one works best for you. Either way, the first step is to cut off all but 1½ inches of the leaf stalk (use a sharp knife or razor blade). Let the cut end heal for two or three hours before burying it in the rooting medium.

If you are rooting leaves in water, submerge 1 inch of the leaf stalk in a shallow dish containing about 2 inches of water and several pieces of charcoal on the bottom. To hold the leaves in place, put a piece of aluminum foil over the container and poke a hole through it for each leaf stem (see illustration on page 35). Transfer leaves to a rooting medium when the roots are ¼ to ½ inch long. You can keep varieties separated by writing the name of each on adhesive tape and sticking it on the leaf. If you are rooting a number of leaves of one variety, use a different container for each, and use wooden or plastic plant labels for markers.

PLASTIC BOXES or aquariums make good containers for rooting African violet leaves. These cuttings are from different varieties and are marked with pieces of tape for identification. Spring is a good time to make cuttings. In foreground is a fresh-cut leaf.

Insert the rooted cutting—or leaf stalk, if you have eliminated the water-rooting step—in the rooting medium to a depth of ¾ inch. (A pencil is useful for making the hole.) If you have several cuttings in one container, space them about 2 inches apart. Place the containers in a warm spot with good light and keep the rooting medium moist.

As the cuttings begin to root, each leaf will probably develop a cluster of small plants. When they are about 1½-2 inches high, it's time to transplant them to pots. Even an expert can't tell you how long it will take the cuttings to reach this stage. It could be three weeks, six weeks, or even longer, depending on the variety and the environment in which it is grown. Under ideal conditions, you could have a blooming plant from a leaf cutting in about six months.

YOUR FIRST PLANTS

You may be a bit bewildered by the array of varieties when you first walk into the greenhouses or salesroom of an African violet grower. Here are some guides to help you make your selection:

Start out with the varieties that have plain leaves; they are much hardier than the fancy, frilled ones. In the plain-leafed types, you'll find both single and double-flowered forms in whites, pinks, blues, purples, and bicolors. Some of the finest of the easy-to-grow varieties are 'Double Black Cherry', a prolific double wine; almost any of the blues ('Wedgewood' and 'Blue Nocturne' are two favorites); 'White Pride Supreme'; 'Gigi' and 'Double Pink Fire', two good double-fringed pinks; 'Wings of Eden', double-fringed blooms of bluish orchid and white; 'Stained Glass', orchid and white; 'King Richard', double-flowered wine bicolor.

If light presents a problem, you will want to remember that the pale-green-leafed varieties with silvery undersides generally require less light than do the darker green foliage types backed with red. Most of the variegated-leaf varieties need strong light in order to maintain the variegation. However, you can convert even the darkest room into a growing area for plants by installing lights specially designed for this purpose (see pages 84-89).

WHEN IT IS TIME TO ADD MORE

Once you have a few African violets and have discovered the ideal growing environment for them, you may want to add some of the fancier kinds to your collection. It is possible to select dozens of plants, each with foliage of a different appearance. There are plain leaves with prominent veining called "quilting." There are large pale green and shiny black-green leaves, particularly attractive because of their ruffled and fluted edges. Some leaves are twisted and curled at the base of the leaf stalk. Other leaves may have scallops along the edges and a large triangle of white at the base—the typical "girl" foliage.

Variegated foliage is becoming more popular, too, although varieties with patterned leaves require special culture to overcome their tendency to revert to plain green. Low light, applications of nitrogenous fertilizer, or too much heat can hasten this reversion. Grow these special plants where temperatures don't go over 70° during the day. Some excellent plants with pink-flecked or blotched, variegated foliage are 'Grand Canyon', 'Silver Carnival', 'Palomino', 'Green Confetti', 'Party Gown', 'Pink Ribbons', 'Happy Ending', and 'Pink 'n Snow'.

In striving for a true red-flowered African violet, hybridizers have developed many new varieties in deep cerise. One of the best, 'Oriental Red', is a bright double on compact tailored foliage. The appearance of plants in seedling blocks with creamy white or chartreuse-edged blooms is a promising trend toward yellow blooms.

For more detailed information on raising African violets, see *Sunset's* book, *How to Grow African Violets.*

THE MINIATURES

If space is your problem, there is a whole group of plants that fall into the miniature class—varieties that stay in 2-inch pots all their lives, never growing over 6 inches in diameter. They are ideal for windowsill gardens, requiring a fair amount of daylight for best growth. Two of the miniatures are 'Baby Roses', a pale-green-leafed form with ½-inch roselike blooms shading from blush on the edges to deep coral pink in the center; and 'Leprechaun', chartreuse-flowered with a wide, bright green ruffled edge and a wine circle around the eye.

'WINTERGREEN' *variety has forest green leaves with chartreuse speckles. Double, pale blue flowers.*

LEAF CUTTINGS *of African violets can be rooted in water. Cover jar with foil, poke holes for stems.*

EPISCIA CUPREATA *has coppery brown and silver leaves. The flowers are red and trumpet-shaped.*

GLOXINIAS AND EPISCIAS

Two relatives of the African violet deserve a place in this chapter—*Sinningia* and *Episcia*. The culture of each is similar to that of African violets, but the habits of growth are somewhat different.

Gloxinias (*Sinningia speciosa*) are grown for their lovely bell-shaped flowers which are sometimes double, ruffled along the edges, and glowing in rich tones of blue, purple, pink, red, or pure white. Some of the blooms are dotted with dark spots; others have blotches of solid colors. The leaves are rich green and velvety to the eye and the touch.

The plants are not difficult to grow but do require a great deal of light (not direct sunlight). They also require high humidity. Fluorescent lights have proved highly successful in growing and flowering these lovely plants. Once in bloom they can be placed anywhere in the house to be enjoyed during their long blooming period. A shaded, protected patio in summer is also a suitable site for these plants.

Plant the tuber (available December-March) 1 inch deep in the same potting soil that you would use for African violets. Water sparingly until the first leaves appear, then increase watering. Don't get water on the leaves; water around the base of the plant or from beneath. Feed on a regular program while plants are in active growth. Repot, moving the plant to a larger pot, when the roots have filled the pot. After the plant has bloomed (take cuttings now; the procedure is the same as for African violets), gradually dry it out. Store the tuber in a cool, dark place, watering just enough to keep the tuber from shriveling. Repot in January or February.

Episcias are often called flame violets. The leaves are similar to those of the African violet except that they are beautifully colored. Some are coppery in color, others are green with white veins, and still others have stripes and different-colored edges. The flowers resemble long-tubed, orange-red African violets. The plant is low-growing with a trailing habit. It spreads by runners much like a strawberry. Episcias are good in hanging baskets, in terrariums, or under fluorescent lights—they require a high humidity. They are easily propagated either by the plantlets or by leaf cuttings. Grow them like African violets.

GLOXINIA with deep blue flowers, white edges. Foliage is deep green, velvety in texture.

TYPICAL DISPLAY in florist's shop. Cart contains violets, gloxinias, ivies, chrysanthemums (floor).

MINIATURE GARDEN *features moss, lichen, parsley fern, and spleenwort.*

TINY FOREST *garden in wooden box has drift-wood, lady fern, red huckleberry, and grasses.*

HOW TO CREATE A MINIATURE GARDEN

During the long winter months, a preview of spring can lift the spirits. You can put together a table-top garden in a shallow bowl and place it where it can be enjoyed by everyone. Collect tiny ferns, grasses, mosses, weeds, and even inch-high seedlings of trees and shrubs wherever you can find them. If the weather outside is cold, the indoor warmth will hasten the unfurling of fronds and the opening of tender green leaves.

The first step in creating your own miniature garden is to select a container; it will determine what size plants you will need. Then take a walk through a wood, a meadow, or even a nearby vacant lot, keeping your eyes open for a few small plants whose form or character arouses your curiosity. Useful tools are a flexible spatula for lifting moss, a stout knife for digging, and a wide flat basket or box in which to carry home your finds. (If you wish to collect in a park or forest, check local regulations first.)

Putting the garden together: Any dish garden you assemble will be easiest to care for and most attractive if it is made up of plants from similar soil and exposure—for example, all woodland plants or all high meadow plants. If you have picked up a lichen-covered rock or piece of weathered wood on your collecting trip, start your garden by placing this first. A layer of small pebbles on the bottom of the bowl will aid drainage. If there is not enough excess soil on the plant roots to fill in and around them in the container, supplement with a mixture of half sand and half peat moss. Then set your plants and firm them in well.

Caring for a dish garden: Watering is the most critical task. With a bulb-type sprayer you can cover every part of the garden without putting an excess of water anywhere. Keep the little garden well groomed, and refresh it occasionally by putting it outdoors when the weather is mild.

INDOOR-OUTDOOR PLANTS

They can improve the scenery, indoors or out

Rotating plants between outdoors and indoors adds a refreshing new dimension to container gardening and a note of surprise to interior decoration. The concept is simple: You have plants that look beautiful in their containers on the terrace, under the roof overhang, near the entry, in the lathhouse. Why not bring them inside for a special occasion—or just to enjoy them up close?

When the weather is cold and outdoor container plants are not getting full attention, it is a good time to try moving some of them indoors. Some plants may stay inside only for an evening, a day, or a weekend. But if the plant is amenable, you may keep it indoors for a week or two, or perhaps for months. Experiment. There is no such thing as a hard-and-fast category of indoor-outdoor plants—any plant you like is a potential candidate. Often such plants are appreciated more fully when brought inside.

AZALEAS massed in straw pot covers make an effective display on a buffet table for a special occasion. Here are pink and white Belgian Indica azaleas. Keep inside while blooming.

LARGE POTTERY bowl contains two camellias, prized for their lovely foliage, flowers.

STEPHANOTIS trained on a wire frame thrives in a sunny spot. Flower fragrance fills the air.

BOUGAINVILLEA is handsome in container by entry window. Stake for support if needed.

GLASS-TOPPED table near a south window is good location for geraniums. Decorative flowers, foliage.

PLANT IN POT may be set in decorative container. Place perlite in bottom to raise plant to rim.

DECORATIVE USES FOR INDOOR-OUTDOOR PLANTS

The possibilities for the attractive use of outdoor plants in the house are almost endless. It would be best for you to experiment with your plants to find what is most pleasing to your eyes. Here are a few suggestions:

Place several pots of golden bamboo on the inside of a glass wall and two or three on the outside. The plants will give the feeling of a green screen—a sense of the garden flowing into the room. The plants can be kept in the house for two or more weeks at a time or until the leaves begin to become dry or start to drop off.

Besides the obvious pleasure of enhancing an interior, bringing plants indoors rewards in other ways. There is the delight of watching a fern frond unfold or of seeing the miraculous opening of a bud or blossom. Potted azaleas brought indoors when the buds first begin to show color will continue to flower for weeks. Blossoms remain more perfect indoors without the spattering and battering of mud, rain, and wind. While the sun slants low and fills the house with winter light, fruiting citrus can prosper. Jade plants can also come indoors for the winter.

An important contribution to the effectiveness of plants placed in the house is made by lighting. A plant placed under a lamp is automatically spotlighted. In the light of a lamp, even such a familiar, old-fashioned plant as coleus or geranium takes on a new aura in which its texture is magnified and its color heightened.

For a party atmosphere, use candles or spotlights. Plants appear glamorous in flickering candlelight. Concealed spotlights create dramatic and theatrical effects on plants or plant groupings.

CONTAINERS

Your choice of containers is almost as wide open as your choice of plants. A handsome plant deserves a handsome container. Ideally the size, shape, color, and texture of a container should relate to the plant as well as to the interior setting. The simpler its design and the less obtrusive its color, the more complementary the container will be to the plant and to its indoor environment.

For a temporary stay indoors, especially if you expect to set it out in the garden shortly, a plant can stay in its nursery can placed inside a larger display container such as large pot, jardiniere, or urn. If the edges of the can protrude above the outside container, make several vertical cuts around the perimeter of the can and bend the edges down until they are no longer visible. Then apply a topdressing of peat moss, ground bark, or similar material to conceal

the can as well as to hold in the moisture. To avoid
water damage to the floor surfaces, set the plant container in a pot saucer or other receptacle.

WHERE TO PLACE PLANTS

The size and shape of the plant and its container will
determine where you should place it. It is often fun
to bring in a huge plant for a special occasion. A
tubbed tree that seems comparatively small outside
will take on giant proportions in a small room and
can add an exciting jungle atmosphere. But ordi-
narily a plant should be more appropriate in size to
the area it occupies.

Plants should relate not only to their backgrounds
but also to other plants and adjacent objects. Combinations of plants seen close up indoors can be just
as satisfying as group plantings in the garden.

Consider the relationship of plants placed on either
side of a window or glass wall. For example, outside
you might feature the delicate texture, yellow-green
color, and look-through quality of bamboo; and inside, for contrast against the background of bamboo,
you might use the bold dark green leaves and the
solid mass of *Fatsia japonica* or *Aucuba japonica*. Or
you might reverse this combination of texture and
color by placing *Camellia japonica* with its dark
green glossy leaves on the outside and a filmy, light
green asparagus fern on the inside.

Plants placed in front of mirrors will give you two
of everything. Emphasize an elegant plant by placing it where it will be reflected in waxed wood, polished marble, or other glossy surface.

GROWTH REQUIREMENTS

Though the growth requirements of outdoor plants
do not change when brought indoors, a few hints as
to indoor care should be helpful.

Light: Light is extremely important. Most plants
kept indoors for any length of time need all the light
you can give them; this applies particularly to plants
whose entire lives have been spent outdoors.

Most outdoor plants will get along best indoors if
you keep them in a cool location near a window. It
will also help to give them additional light from a
lamp, especially during the winter period of limited
daylight.

Of course, plants that normally grow outdoors in
shade or partial shade (such as most ferns, aucuba,
or fatsia) will succeed with less light. Even a few
succulents, notably dudleya and gasteria, take low
light conditions over long periods. But remember
that a plant accustomed to growing in shade outdoors will burn if you expose it to full sun shining
through a window facing west or south. In fact, even

PALMS (Chamaedorea seifrizii) · *indoors and out
seem to blend the two areas into one.*

GARDEN ROOM *shows collection of plants to best
advantage. Shelves are slatted, made of wood.*

REDDISH PURPLE, *lacy leaves of Japanese maple make the tree an interesting container subject.*

NORFOLK ISLAND PINE *in a wooden box has ostrich-plume-like branches.*

sun-tolerant plants need protection from the extreme heat created by sunlight shining through clear glass.

Water and humidity: The atmosphere in many homes is too warm and dry for plants, particularly for plants normally grown outdoors. To overcome this handicap, follow the usual procedure for regular house plants. Place the container on a layer of pebbles in a deep saucer or pan. Barely cover the pebbles with water; as it evaporates, it will release moisture into the atmosphere around the plant (see page 30).

ENCYCLOPEDIA

Earlier in this chapter the suggestion was made that any plant may be tried as an indoor-outdoor plant. The list that follows is intended to give you further suggestions as to the possibilities for indoor-outdoor plant surprises. Watch carefully for signs that the plant or plants should be returned outside.

Abutilon (flowering maple): Grown mostly for flowers. Bring indoors in cold climate areas in winter; leave out on the patio in summer. Pinch branch tips often to control rangy growth. Needs moist soil, partial shade.

Acer palmatum (Japanese maple): Bright red autumn foliage. Airy, delicate growth habit for all-year interest. Likes same conditions as azaleas—ample water, periodic feeding, protection from heat. Bring indoors only briefly. (This applies to all small maples in containers.)

African linden: See *Sparmannia africana*

Araucaria heterophylla (Norfolk Island pine): Young leaves are narrow, ½ inch long, and curved with sharp points. Mature leaves are more triangular and overlapping. Grows in a pyramidal shape. Can be grown outdoors in mild climates, indoors or indoors-outdoors elsewhere.

Azalea: Spectacular when in bloom. Bring inside when buds form and keep inside while flowering. Then return to outdoors. Keep moist but not soggy, and feed with acid plant food every 6-8 weeks, 3 or 4 times from the end of flowering season until September. Prune at blooming time and pinch back new tips to keep plant bushy.

Bamboo: Many kinds of bamboo can be grown in containers and brought into the house for short periods. You might consider having two containers of bamboo that you can alternate. Feed and fertilize regularly and repot every 2-3 years. The following bamboos adapt well to containers:

Bambusa multiplex riviereorum (Chinese goddess bamboo): Graceful growth habit. Stems ½ inch thick bear small leaves in ferny sprays; reaches height of 4-6 feet.

Phyllostachys aurea (golden bamboo): Dense foliage on stems 6-10 feet high. Water frequently.

P. nigra (black bamboo): Stems vary from pure black to olive-dotted black. Grows to 4-8 feet. Protect from hot afternoon sun.

P. viridis: Curving, tall stems bearing ferny growth at base. Good for narrow areas. Reaches 15-20 feet.

Sasa palmata (palmate bamboo): Unbamboo-like appearance. Handsome, broad leaves spread finger-like from stems. Will reach 4-5 feet.

Bamburanta: See *Ctenanthe compressa*

Beloperone guttata (shrimp plant): Common name derived from tubular flowers covered with coppery bronze bracts that resemble large shrimp. Interesting bushy plant—pinch back to keep shape. Keep inside in winter, outside on terrace, patio, or entryway when weather is mild.

Bird of paradise: See *Strelitzia reginae*

Black bamboo: See bamboo

Bonsai: Any bonsai may be brought inside for short periods to be used as an accent. Watch closely for signs of dropping leaves or needles. Keep inside only briefly.

Bougainvillea: Vibrant red color. Use bushy forms. Bring in when temperature threatens at 30°. Use basic potting mix, feed spring and summer. Prune to shape the plant.

Camellia: Lovely flowers and handsome foliage. Pot in acid mix, feed with acid food after bloom. Bring inside for a week or more, longer in a cool, light atrium, lanai, or garden room.

Chinese goddess bamboo: See bamboo

Chrysanthemum: These plants can be brought inside and enjoyed while in bloom, then returned outdoors and either planted in the garden or allowed to remain in the pot. Do not allow to become potbound. Cut off faded flowers. When new shoots show at base, cut off remainder of old flower stem.

Citrus: Dwarf varieties make excellent indoor-outdoor plants. Glossy evergreen foliage, fragrant blossoms, colorful fruit make them ideal container trees. Water daily in hot weather; fertilize with high-nitrogen (citrus) fertilizer in late winter, June, and August. Choose from kumquat, lemon, lime, mandarin orange, orange, 'Rangpur' lime, and tangelo.

Ctenanthe compressa (bamburanta): Plants grow to 2-3 feet high with leathery oblong leaves on wiry stems. Grown mostly for leaves. Grow in partial shade in rich, moist soil. Feed regularly. Combines well with other foliage plants.

BLACK BAMBOO *planted in square black box set on pebble-filled tray. Needs bright light.*

HIBISCUS will bloom well indoors during the winter months. Return outdoors when the weather warms.

EXOTIC BIRD OF PARADISE provides tropical note. Flowers of blue, orange, white resemble birds.

Fatshedera lizei: Vine that climbs like ivy. Plant is shrubby in habit, heavy, and needs support. Likes partial shade. Cut back if it gets too large.

Fern pine: See *Podocarpus gracilior*

Flowering maple: See *Abutilon*

Gardenia: Grown for lovely, fragrant, white flowers. Glossy, dark green foliage is also attractive. Needs warm days and nights and moist, well draining soil. Feed every 3-4 weeks with acid fertilizer.

Golden bamboo: See bamboo

Hibiscus: Prized for its lovely 4 to 8-inch-wide flowers, which may be single or double. Colors range from white through pink to red, from yellow and apricot to orange. Glossy foliage. Height varies. Plants require good drainage, frequent watering, twice monthly feeding. Bring inside when temperatures go below 30°. Plants need sun and heat, but protect them from wind. Pinch back to encourage flowering.

Japanese maple: See *Acer palmatum*

Kumquat: See *Citrus*

Lemon: See *Citrus*

Lime: See *Citrus*

Mahonia lomariifolia: Interesting branch structure with spiny, glossy leaves. Yellow flowers are followed by berries which have a powdery blue coating. Good in an entry or narrow area—but watch out for spines, for they will scratch or catch clothing.

Mandarin orange: See *Citrus*

Norfolk Island pine: See *Araucaria heterophylla*

Orange: See *Citrus*

Podocarpus gracilior (fern pine): Gray or blue-green narrow leaves closely spaced on branches. Seedlings good for dish gardens. As plants mature, they become upright—a single or multiple stemmed tree.

P. macrophyllus maki (shrubby yew pine): Good for indoor-outdoor use. Grows slowly to 6-8 feet. Leaves 3 inches long, ¼ inch wide, bright green. Grows in an upright form.

'Rangpur' lime: See *Citrus*

Shrimp plant: See *Beloperone guttata*

Sparmannia africana (African linden): Dense, coarse foliage. Leaves to 9 inches across, light green, heavily veined, with velvety texture. Grows into many trunks from base. Grows in either sun or shade. Water and feed well. Bring indoors in winter. Combine with other tropical plants; furnishes bulk and mass.

Strelitzia reginae (bird of paradise): Startling flowers of orange, blue, and white resemble tropical birds. Feed frequently and heavily. Divide infrequently, since crowded conditions produce better flowers.

Tangelo: See *Citrus*

Yew pine: See *Podocarpus macrophyllus maki*

IN SUMMER *a sunny terrace or patio is best place for geraniums. Bring indoors during winter.*

RED-LEAFED *Ethiopian banana (Ensete maurelii) can be indoor-outdoor plant in mild-climate areas.*

MAHONIA LOMARIIFOLIA *against glass panel in entry. Also could be used on outer side.*

FUCHSIAS make good indoor-outdoor plants. Shown here is the hanging type in a lathhouse.

ARALIA decorated with sparkling tiny lights. This is a good idea for the holidays—inside or out.

SEEDLING BONSAI of Japanese maple adds a note of grace. Keep inside only for brief periods.

SMALL CITRUS make delightful gifts, require same care as most house plants.

VIEW *through bedroom window. Garden contains azalea, jade plant, wisteria, stone figure.*

GARDEN *off dining room contains pines, ivy, hydrangea, geranium, jade plant, bronze figure.*

WHEN SPACE IS AT A PREMIUM

Ingenious home owners with limited space have designed many ways to display and grow their collections of container plants. Illustrated on this page are three examples. There are many possibilities, and perhaps you can come up with a unique idea to suit your own purpose and location.

The window garden illustrated at the right is an old store showcase which was modified to become a delightful kitchen window garden. It provides 8 square feet of growing space (4 feet wide by 2 feet deep) and stands 33 inches high, from sill to top.

After a new 12-inch-deep base was made for it, a tinsmith fitted a metal liner inside. This made it possible to fill the base with soil and grow plants directly inside. The liner is vented to drain outdoors. Plants in containers could also be grown in such a garden.

Small-leafed ivies, African violets, gloxinias, and cyclamen have been grown successfully here. Chives, parsley, and a few herbs are always growing near the front of the window garden where they are handy for snipping.

Although the case faces south, a tree in the garden shades it in summer from all except early morning sun.

The other two gardens illustrated in the photographs on this page are built on roofs. Enclosed with plastic panels set in redwood frames, the two spaces were transformed into garden rooms ideally suited for the display of choice container plants and various Oriental objects. The gardens also provide the house interior with privacy from neighboring houses.

WINDOW GARDEN *rests on sill, corner supports.*

SUCCULENTS AND CACTUS

A fascinating array in form and color

Generally speaking, all plants that have water storage mechanisms are succulents, and such plants can be found in many different families. For example, there are succulents in the daisy family and the lily family. Cactus are succulents, but because they are so special they deserve to be singled out for addi-tional attention. Since these plants have become modified to store water, they can withstand long periods without rain. This is a clue to the culture of the plants. If you don't have much time or patience for plants, cactus and succulents may be the answer. They thrive on warm, dry conditions with little water.

INGENIOUS DISPLAY IDEA: *bench with gravel section for plants. Top row, left to right:* echeveria hybrid, Sempervivum arachnoideum. *Lower row:* Echeveria elegans *and* S. tectorum.

THIS GASTERIA *started three years ago from section now grows in an old pewter creamer.*

EFFECTIVE *grouping of cactus on a low bench. The arrangement is striking because of its simplicity.*

CRASSULA ARGENTEA *is a handsome succulent. Planted at the base is* Aeonium canariense.

SILVERY WHITE SUCCULENT (Cotyledon) *grows well near east-facing glass wall.*

DECORATIVE USES FOR SUCCULENTS AND CACTUS

Succulents can be used much as other types of house plants. Several different kinds can be combined in one decorative pot for variation. Many succulents have lovely flowers and will provide a delightful accent for any room.

CONTAINERS

Small containers are best for succulents. For plants of a rounded form, use a pot 1 inch wider than the diameter of the plant. For tall-growing plants, select a pot half as wide as the plant is tall. Unglazed, standard clay pots are preferable, but glazed containers are satisfactory if drainage is well provided. Plastic pots can also be used, but take care not to overwater.

GROWTH CHARACTERISTICS

There are cactus and succulents in almost all sizes and shapes. Many are so large that they are not suitable for even garden culture, but there is a large and diverse group that can be used for indoor culture. One example is the living stones—cactus that really look like stones until you see them in flower. Shapes as well as colors vary, so with wise buying you can have quite an assortment of forms in the plants as well as in the flowers. Children are especially fond of cactus because of their unique growth and flowering habits.

GROWTH REQUIREMENTS

Succulents are nearly perfect container plants. They are easy to plant, easy to grow, good looking all year, and long-lasting. Many kinds can be grown either indoors or outdoors, or both. A few simple guidelines will help you to have success with your succulents.

Temperature: In the summer when the light is bright, most cactus and succulents can take any amount of heat. However, in the cooler months when the light is poor even on a windowsill, average home temperature is adequate.

Light: Direct sunlight is fine in the summer. This is the period of active growth. On some of the brightest summer days a light curtain may be necessary to prevent burning of some of the more tender varieties. Windowsill culture is also suitable in the winter. If plants are to be moved outdoors in the summer, some more tender kinds will not take full sun.

Water: Before watering, use a match stick to scratch down a half inch into the potting medium. If the soil appears dry at that depth, water the plant

GREENHOUSE collection of a wide variety of succulents. Most of them do well as house plants.

thoroughly from the top of the pot. Soaking the pot in a pan of water or wetting the foliage continually may rot succulents.

In summer, succulents may only need water once a week; if the weather is cool and moist, they may need it only once every two or three weeks. When the weather turns cool in the fall, water just enough to keep them from shriveling. In March or April when the plants start making new growth, gradually increase watering. The winter rest is necessary in order to produce flowers the next spring. These rules are meant only as guidelines. Check to see if the plants need water; do not water completely on a set time schedule.

Fertilizing: If using a well balanced potting soil with fertilizer added, there is no need for you to add more the first year. The second year a monthly application of a well balanced, dilute fertilizer once a month will be beneficial.

Ventilation: Good ventilation is desirable with succulents as with all other house plants.

Pests, diseases, and control: Taking all precautions to avoid infestations or disease is the best control measure. Buy only healthy plants. If there is evidence of pests, consult the chapter on Pests and Diseases, pages 81-83.

LOPSIDED SUCCULENT, jade plant, is too tall for container, and one branch is too long.

SANDY MIX

3 CUBIC FEET

1¹/₂ cubic feet organic matter

1¹/₂ cubic feet sandy soil or sand

³/₄ pound dry complete fertilizer
(see page 16)

2 pounds limestone

(Organic matter may vary according to regional availability—ground bark, peat moss, rice hulls, and others.)

Mix ingredients thoroughly and store in covered containers for future use.

Note: You can buy prepared mixes or use your own favorite mix as long as it is porous, drains well but retains moisture, and contains some nutrients.

CAREFUL and selective pruning brings symmetry to plant. Lower structure is also revealed.

1. *LEAF CUTTINGS. Cut outside leaf with shears. Two small plants at base can be separated.*

2. *CUT leaf into small pieces, marking tops. Let dry for week, then insert bottoms in sand.*

POTTING AND REPOTTING

Succulents and cactus should be repotted every two years. The best time to do this is in the spring when the plants begin active growth. These plants do not have much of a root system so it may be necessary to anchor the plant in the pot until the plant becomes rooted in the new medium. For large plants, place a stake in the pot and tie plant to stake. For small plants, fasten with two rubber bands or pieces of string as in photograph on page 54.

Pot as you would any other plant, using the soil mixture described on page 51. Place a piece of broken pot, curved side up, over the drainage hole, then add potting mix and plant, tapping pot to settle and firm the soil. Water sparingly until the plant starts to root, then increase watering.

PROPAGATION

Propagating succulents from cuttings is one of the most rewarding projects for the home gardener. In fact, once you have been bitten by the succulent bug, you may find it hard to stop adding to your collection.

You can tell pretty much by looking at a succulent how best to propagate it. If it is a shrublike plant such as the jade plant *(Crassula argentea)* or *Aeonium* 'Cooperi', you should probably take tip cuttings. If the plant looks as if it's nothing but a lot of long leaves, such as sansevieria, then make leaf cuttings. If in doubt, try all the methods—a tip cutting, a leaf, a leafy flower stalk. Some cactus and succulents also produce offsets, which simplifies propagation.

One of the most critical steps in making a successful succulent cutting is to allow the end of the cutting to callus. This callusing or drying is a crucial step in the vegetative propagation of succulents. Fresh cuttings are likely to rot. Let the tip cuttings dry for one to two weeks in a warm, shady spot. Leaf cuttings dry faster and can usually be planted in about a week.

The best cuttings are made from mature growth, rather than new, tender tips or leaves. If you want big plants and don't want to wait too long for flowers, take good-sized cuttings.

Builder's sand has long been a favorite rooting medium for succulents. Some specialists now have their own mixes, but sand is readily available and still a safe bet. Insert a callused cutting into dry sand just deep enough so it doesn't topple over; use a pot, flat, or box. Set the container in a warm, shady spot until the cutting is rooted. Water just enough to keep the cutting from shriveling up.

Tip cuttings root and start to grow with little or no shriveling of the old leaves, but leaf cuttings from most succulents dry up to almost nothing as the new plant at the base forms and grows.

Once the new plant has formed roots ¾-1 inch long, move it into a larger container (when using pots it is best to move it into a pot one size larger), or put hardy kinds into garden beds. Put more tender types in the garden only for the summer. (See box on page 51 for instructions regarding the potting mixture.)

Grafting: It is easy to graft one kind of cactus (the scion) onto another kind of cactus (the stock). It is easier than grafting deciduous fruit trees, roses, and camellias because when you graft a cactus you make quick slices through relatively soft tissues instead of sawing through woody tissue.

Also, you don't have to worry about compatability of stock and scion as you do with deciduous fruit trees. Most cactus scions will grow on any cactus stock, as long as both are healthy and vigorous. It is easier, too, because in grafting fruit trees, you must follow the tricky and difficult technique of lining up the growth layers near the outside of stock and scion; with cactus you simply match the cut tissues of stock and scion or, if you can, line up inner growth rings (darker circles in the core of the plant).

There are several good reasons for grafting cactus:

1. Grafting encourages faster growth and earlier bloom on slow-growing forms.

2. The rare and highly prized crests, which are abnormally flattened or twisted growths at the tops of cactus stems, usually don't last long. You can keep crests growing for many years if you graft them onto a strong rootstock.

3. You can graft a cactus that roots easily onto a tall rootstock to keep it above the moist ground.

4. If a choice cactus becomes diseased, you can usually save it—if you act quickly—by removing infected tissue and grafting the healthy part onto a vigorous rootstock.

5. Smaller forms grafted on a tall rootstock make the plants more prominent in the bed or container.

6. You can make an attractive standard, or treelike plant, by grafting a weeping cactus onto a slender-stemmed stock.

The best time to graft cactus is in late spring or in summer. Some experts recommend grafting cactus only on a warm, sunny day when the plant sap is moving rapidly in the rootstock and scion.

You'll need the following tools and supplies for grafting cactus: tongs or several thick cloths to hold spiny plants; a high quality steel knife with razor-sharp edge; a pair of shears to trim spines; rubber bands and spines to hold stock and scion together; a small brush for dusting on sulfur; and a paper bag.

When making the graft, be sure matching surfaces

1. LEGGY ECHEVERIA can be cut off and the stem inserted in sand. Base will grow small plants.

2. INSERT 1½-inch stem in sand in can. The head will keep light out. Roots form in 3 weeks.

1. FLAT GRAFT *made by cutting stock transversely. Trim shoulders as shown. Keep all exposed surfaces clean. This stock is* Trichocereus spachianus.

2. MATCH *inner growth rings of stock and scion. Secure scion in place with rubber bands. Place paper bag over graft; should knit in 5 to 7 days.*

1. CLEFT GRAFT. *Cut top of stock and make cleft as shown. Cut scion to fit cleft. Use rubber bands and spines to hold scion in place.*

2. SCION *secured to stock with spines. Use this graft for making standards of weeping forms such as Easter cactus as used above.*

A COLLECTION of grafts of choice cactus plants and the twisted and fan-shaped growth of rare crests. These plants grow faster and bloom earlier when they are grafted on a strong rootstock. Use your imagination in combining rootstock and scion.

of stock and scion are perfectly smooth and clean. Slice to make cuts—never use a sawing motion with the knife. Place cut surfaces together as quickly as possible. The slightest drying out of either surface to be matched will end in failure of the graft.

After the graft is in place, dust the exposed cut surfaces with sulfur to prevent disease and to encourage rapid healing. Cover graft with a paper bag for several days to protect it from dirt and dryness while stock and scion are uniting.

Use care when moving or watering grafted cactus. A sudden jar may loosen the graft and allow entrance of disease. If water splashes on the graft, it may encourage rot at the graft union.

The photographs on the opposite page illustrate the grafting procedure.

ENCYCLOPEDIA

It would be impossible to list all of the succulents that are adaptable for culture as house plants. The list that follows, however, will introduce you to this fascinating group of plants. You can go on from here.

Aeonium: Useful succulents for decorative effects. Leaves in rosettes in bright green or dark purple, often red edged. Flowers in yellow or white.

Agave: Mostly gigantic. Several smaller forms suitable for pots. *A. victoriae-reginae* has narrow, dark green leaves with white lines. Leaves are 6 inches long and 2 inches wide. Some of the larger forms can be kept smaller in pots by watering and feeding less frequently. Try *A. stricta, A. filifera.*

Air plant: See *Kalanchoe pinnata*

Aloe: Succulents of the lily family. Clumps of fleshy, pointed leaves and clusters of orange, yellow, or red flowers. Showy and easy to grow.

Barrel cactus: See *Ferocactus*

Chamaecereus silvestri (peanut cactus): Small, cylindrical, ribbed, and spiny. Joints, 2-3 inches long, fall off easily and will root easily. Blooms freely in spring and early summer. Flowers are 3 inches long and bright red in color.

Chollas: See *Opuntia*

Christmas cactus: See *Schlumbergera*

Coryphantha vivipara: Little cactus. Has single or clustered globular bodies covered with knobs that bear white spines. Flowers are purple and showy.

Cotyledon: Many sizes and appearances. Some are shrubby. Attractive flowers, mostly in clusters, in many colors.

Crassula: Most popular is *C. argentea* (jade plant), stout trunk and sturdy limbs even on small plants.

CRASSULA is shown here in full bloom, but it may not flower as house plant.

Leaves are thick, oblong fleshy pads, 1-2 inches long of glossy, bright green color often edged with red. Clusters of pink flowers in profusion from November to April. (There are many other species, some with interesting geometrical forms, others with brilliant flowers.)

Easter cactus: See *Rhipsalidopsis*

Echeveria: All make attractive rosettes of fleshy leaves. Colored green or gray-green and often marked or overlaid with deeper colors. Bell-shaped flowers borne on stalks above rosettes.

Echinopsis: Cactus. Many kinds, all showy and easy to grow. Small cylindrical or globular with long-tubed, many-petaled flowers in shades of yellow, pink, or red. Free blooming in the summer if given good light and frequent feedings.

Epiphyllum (orchid cactus): Mostly epiphytic. These plants grow natively in rich, moist soil in part shade, so their culture differs from that of most other succulents and cactus. Stems are long, flat, smooth, and usually notched along the edges. Flowers range from medium to very large in wide range of colors. Bloom season is April to June.

Euphorbia: Large group of plants, many of which are succulents. Most have a milky sap which can irritate the skin. Flowers are usually small and not striking. (Crown of thorns and poinsettias also belong in this family.)

Ferocactus (barrel cactus): Mostly globular with ridges and spines. Some are cylindrical. Flowers in many shades of yellow. Spines often colored. Some kinds grow quite large with age, but there are many smaller ones suitable for pot culture.

Gasteria: Many rosette forms. Others have thick, tongue-shaped leaves spirally arranged. Many are beautifully marked and spotted. Spikes of showy blooms.

Haworthia: Variable growth habit. Many with small rosettes of interestingly marked leaves. Flowers in spikelike clusters.

Hen and chickens: See *Sempervivum*

Jade plant: See *Crassula*

Kalanchoe: Shapes and sizes varied. Flowers fairly large, bell-shaped, brightly colored in a few species. Maternity plant (*K. daigremontiana*) has notched leaf edges. In these notches young plants sprout and even root. Air plant (*K. pinnata*) also produces plantlets on leaves. A leaf pinned to a curtain will produce plantlets until it dries up.

Lithops: Among the best known of the "living rocks" or "pebble plants." Shaped like an inverted cone; top shaped like a stone with a fissure across the middle. Large flowers and new leaves emerge from the fissure. Many species, all interesting.

Living rocks: See *Lithops*

AGAVE PICTA, smaller and daintier than many agaves, has rosette of long leaves, edged white.

Lobivia: Cactus. Globular or cylindrical in shape. Large, showy flowers in shades of red, yellow, pink, orange, purplish lilac. Many species.

Lobivopsis: Cactus. Big flowers on small plants. Similar to *Lobivia* and *Echinopsis.* Grow in good-sized pots (5-inch pot for a 3-inch plant). Many hybrids in lovely colors.

Mammillaria: Cactus. Small, cylindrical or globe-shaped, either single-stemmed or clustered. Flowers are small and arranged in a circle near the top of the plant—red, pink, yellow, or white. Many species.

Maternity plant: See *Kalanchoe*

Notocactus: Usual shape is a small globe; a few are columns. All are covered with spines. Lovely flowers in many colors.

Opuntia: Cactus. Many kinds with varied appearance, often bizarre. Most species fall into 1 of 2 categories: those having flat, broad joints; or those having cylindrical joints. The first are called prickly pears and the second chollas (these are rather loose categories). Flowers are large and showy in yellow, orange, or red.

Orchid cactus: See *Epiphyllum*

Peanut cactus: See *Chamaecereus silvestri*

Pebble plants: See *Lithops*

Pleiospilos (split rock): Has 1 or 2 pairs of leaves that resemble gray or gray-green rounded pebbles. Flowers are large and resemble those of ice plants.

Prickly pears: See *Opuntia*

Rhipsalidopsis (Easter cactus): Similar to the Christmas cactus (also epiphytic), but plant is more upright. Flowers to 3 inches long, bright red, rather drooping. Blooms April, May, and often again in September. Many varieties in shades of red or pink.

Schlumbergera: Cactus. Epiphytic plants in nature. Water frequently and feed often. *S. bridgesii* is the favorite Christmas cactus with its lovely tubular flowers at Christmas time.

Sedum: Some tiny and trailing, others upright. Leaves are fleshy, highly variable in size, shape, and color. Flowers are small in fairly large clusters, sometimes brightly colored.

Sempervivum: Tightly packed rosettes of leaves. Little offsets cluster around parent rosette. Flowers in clusters are not showy. *S. tectorum* is the familiar hen and chickens.

Split rock: See *Pleiospilos*

Stapelia: Often called carrion flowers. Small, spineless, 4-sided stems bear large, star-shaped flowers that often are unpleasantly odorous.

Trichocereus: Cactus. Columnar, sometimes branched with ridges and spines. Large flowers usually white; night blooming and very fragrant.

ECHEVERIA ELEGANS complements a fancy egg cup. A good addition for a young girl's room.

'MISSION BELL' orchid cactus has long, pointed buds that open into brilliant orange-red flowers.

SMALL GARDEN *created by a child. Jade plant forms the 'tree' which is set off by marble chips.*

JADE PLANT *provides accent for a collection of stoneware bowls and tile on the end of a bench.*

A COFFEE TABLE *with a marble top makes a background for two small, blooming cactus plants.*

SEDUM REFLEXUM CRISTATUM *forms lush green mat. Yellow flowers bloom on long stems.*

Children can grow many plants from food items normally kept in the kitchen supply cabinet or refrigerator. The resulting enjoyment and feeling of accomplishment for the young gardener can have no measure. The following ideas are intended to be suggestions and are by no means a complete list. Success in some of the following ventures can open new horizons for the budding enthusiast.

The root crops will provide a variety of foliage from lacy to bold, and in all shades of green. Cut off the root, leaving an inch. Trim off the old top leaves. Try carrots, beets, turnips, rutabagas, parsnips, horseradish. Root them in sand.

Sweet potatoes will grow lovely vines if treated in the following manner: Place toothpicks in the sides of the potato and rest them on the rim of a glass containing water, so that the tapered end of the potato is down and about a third is in water. A hyacinth glass is a good container for rooting and growing the vine. Select a sweet potato with signs of life in the eyes.

An avocado seed will grow into a lovely plant to be used in the house. Treat it much the same as the sweet potato with the lower part in water. When roots have formed (in about two months), add soil to the water to about half-and-half proportions. After about two weeks of this treatment, carefully pot the avocado plant.

The seeds of all citrus fruits can be planted in soil in pots or other containers and will grow into little trees. Growth will be increased if a little liquid fertilizer is added after the seeds have sprouted.

Lentils which you purchase from the grocery store can also be planted in soil and will soon sprout. You can create your own Jack-in-the-beanstalk.

The next time you purchase a pineapple, slice off the top, leaving about 2 inches of the fruit on it. Place the top in sand to root. When a good root system has formed, plant the pineapple in good moist soil. You now have a bromeliad.

Natural sponges (not the synthetic ones) can be implanted with the seeds of grass or clover. The sponge should be kept moist. Keep it on a saucer or hang it in a wire basket for a green "ball."

GARDEN *created with potato as "mountain." Small boats sail on the "lake."*

A COMPLETE *garden scene should be fertilized biweekly to keep plants thriving.*

BROMELIADS

Prized for their show-stopper qualities

Attractive in form and foliage throughout the year and easy to grow as house plants, bromeliads make a very attractive addition to house plant collections. Some have broad leaves, others grasslike ones. Blooms, carried in low clusters in the heart of the plants or on tall spikes, often last two to six months. Blossoms are often not spectacular, but they are sometimes followed by colorful "berries" that hang on for months after the blossoms fade. Others carry their flowers in colorful flower heads. In some cases, some or all of the leaves will take on bright colors when the plant is in bloom. Bloom season may vary from year to year and from variety to variety.

Most wild bromeliads grow on rocks or trees as epiphytes (plants that derive their moisture and nourishment from the air and from debris that lodges in crevices or tree limbs). Orchids are epiphytes, but unlike most orchids, bromeliads grow well in the dry atmosphere of the house and thrive in a variety of porous, fast-draining potting mixes. The other type of bromeliad is called terrestrial (a plant that grows in the ground). There are some bromeliads that adapt themselves as terrestrials and epiphytes. Most bromeliads will readily adapt to home conditions and will survive more neglect than will other house plants. The plants grow naturally in tropical America and are found in increasing numbers and varieties at local nurseries and at some florists'.

AECHMEA FASCIATA is a striking plant for an end table or coffee table. The leaves are gray-green, striped with silvery white. Flower spike is cluster of pink bracts around blue flowers.

AECHMEA CHANTINII *has olive to brownish green leaves barred with silver; note new plantlet.*

NEOREGELIA CAROLINAE *'Tricolor', green and white striped leaves that turn pink toward center.*

VRIESIA SPLENDENS *'Major' has dark green leaves banded purple. Flaming sword is red.*

MATERIALS FOR BROMELIAD TREE: 1, *container;* 2, *branch;* 3, *pebbles;* 4, *1 lb. plaster of Paris;* 5, *stones;* 6, ¼ *lb. sphagnum moss;* 7, *galvanized wire;* 8, *several bromeliad plants.*

PLACE *branch at desired angle and anchor with stones. Add heavy mix of plaster; cover with pebbles. Wrap roots of plants with sphagnum moss.*

TO FINISH *tree, arrange plants with larger ones nearer base, smaller ones above. Wire each of the plants in place.*

DECORATIVE USES FOR BROMELIADS

Bromeliads are striking; a single plant placed on a coffee table can provide a very interesting accent for the living room. They can also be used effectively on a terrace or patio. An arrangement of epiphytic bromeliads on an attractive piece of driftwood can be exciting. This is the way they often grow on trees in nature.

The roots of most of the tree-borne bromeliads serve principally to anchor the plants; the water is often stored in cuplike leaf rosettes. The plants will do well on your tree if the cups are kept filled with water and the leaves are occasionally sprayed with water. Syringe the sphagnum moss weekly. See photographs on page 62 for detailed instructions on how to construct your bromeliad tree.

CONTAINERS

Clay pots seem to work best for bromeliads though plastic ones can be used. However, since the plastic pots are lighter there may be a tendency for the plants to be topheavy. Also watch your watering habits with the plastic pots, as the potting medium will not dry out as quickly and may become soggy if overwatered.

A 4 to 5-inch pot size is recommended for bromeliads, even the larger ones. These plants do not have much of a root system so a large pot is not required. Fill the pot ⅓ full of pebbles or broken pot, then add potting mix. Place plant on the mix and work mix carefully around the roots, taking care not to place the plant too deeply in the pot. Staking may be necessary until the roots take hold. Orchid slabs or tree fern will also serve as a suitable base for bromeliads. Follow the directions for anchoring the plant given for constructing the bromeliad tree.

GROWTH CHARACTERISTICS

Bromeliads grow in many forms. By far the most common form is a vase or bowl type—the leaves form a rosette with a small vase in the center that contains water. Where the plants grow naturally in the tropics, debris, insects, and sometimes even frogs make their homes there and many eventually die and provide fertilizer for the plants. In some cases the rosette forms a tall vase, while in others the rosette is much flattened. New leaves are formed from the center so that the outer lower ones eventually discolor and dry out. Remove these to improve the appearance of the plant.

Some bromeliads can be forced into bloom if the plant is large enough. Place an apple in the center of the plant and cover the entire plant with a plastic bag. Allow the plant to remain in the bag for four days and then remove the bag and the apple. The plant should bloom in two to three months. (It is the ethylene gas produced by the apple that initiates the flower buds.)

Another form of bromeliad is the tubular one—some billbergias are an example of this type of growth. Most bromeliads do not have extensive root systems, so a porous, well drained soil is important. These plants are also adaptable to growing on slabs of bark or being used to create a bromeliad tree (see photographs on page 62).

POTTING MIX FOR BROMELIADS

EPIPHYTES

1 part	soil	
1 part	coarse river sand	
1 part	peat moss	
½ part	crushed granite or fir bark or osmunda	

TERRESTRIALS

1 part	leafmold
1 part	manure
1 part	sand
	Small amount of crushed rock

Note: Use your favorite soil mix as long as it is porous and fast draining.

GROWTH REQUIREMENTS

The name bromeliad has an exotic ring and therefore may seem to have difficult growth requirements. However, these plants are quite simple to grow; their needs are discussed in this section.

Bromeliads combine well with ferns, orchids, philodendrons, and begonias. Two familiar members of the family are the pineapple and Spanish moss (the latter being a bromeliad without roots).

Temperature: Native to the tropical regions of North, Central, and South America, bromeliads tolerate temperatures from 130° right down to freezing, depending on the species, but most perform best between 50° and 70°.

Light: Grow bromeliads in a fast-draining but moisture-retentive soil (see box on page 63) in which air can circulate freely around the roots. Most bromeliads produce their best bloom and most colorful foliage when grown in locations that receive plenty of light. However, to prevent the burning of foliage and flowers of the more tender kinds, shade them from the hot sun. These plants can be moved out of doors in the summer months if you pick a shady, protected location.

Water: Many bromeliads have a water-holding cup formed by the arrangement of the leaves. To prevent plants from wilting, sprinkle with a hose or hand mist sprayer once or twice a week to keep these cups full. Water thoroughly around the roots when the soil mix is dry to the touch. There are a few exceptions to this rule. In general, guzmanias, nidulariums, and neoregelias should not be allowed to dry out. These plants grow natively in very moist places.

Ventilation: In nature bromeliads are found in places where the air circulates freely. Fresh air is essential for good growth, but avoid drafts.

AECHMEA PENDULIFLORA has green-tipped, whitish berries that later turn pink, then blue.

Fertilizing: Feed bromeliads regularly with a liquid plant food that is diluted to half the normally recommended strength. If you grow a kind that has cups, fill them with the same dilute solution.

Pests, diseases, and control: If plants are attacked by mealybugs, scale, or spider mites or aphids, spray with malathion. Bait for slugs and snails, especially if you put plants outdoors in summer. (See chapter on Pests and Diseases on pages 81-83.)

PROPAGATION

Shoots that grow off from the side of the main crown of foliage (technically and reasonably called offshoots) can easily be removed to start new plants. Wait until base of the offshoot is hard and woody before attempting to remove it; soft, succulent growth is vulnerable to rot.

To remove offshoots, break them carefully but firmly from the main stem, or cut them off with a sharp knife as close to the main stem of the parent plant as possible. Plant the offshoots in 3 or 3½-inch pots, moving them on to a 4 or 5-inch size when they become rootbound. They will usually produce flowering plants one to two years after separation from their parent. The original plant will not bloom again.

Some genera produce offshoots close to the flowering cup and eventually choke off the mother plant. Others send shoots from the axils of the leaves at the top of the cup. These can be pinched off when large enough to pot. Most bromeliads produce offshoots after flowering though some will produce them before or during this period.

ENCYCLOPEDIA

Included in the following list is a wide range of bromeliads. There are many more, however.

Aechmea chantinii: Olive to brownish green leaves barred with silver. The flower cluster has yellowish blooms, orange-red, red, or pink bracts tipped yellow and white. The plant has the vase form of growth.

A. fasciata: Green leaves banded white, with a powdery coating. The long-lasting flower clusters have numerous blue flowers that change to deep rose with age. The bracts are pink. These have vase form of growth.

A. fulgens discolor: Green leaves backed with purple. The flowers are red tipped with blue and are followed by berries that are a rose color and last about 3 months.

A. penduliflora: Strap-shaped, glossy green leaves turn to maroon in strong light. Branching clusters of yellow flowers above red bracts appear on tall, lean-

CRYPTANTHUS ZONATUS 'ZEBRINUS'. *Foliage is stiff, reddish bronze in color with silver crossbands. White flowers in a small cluster are formed in the center of the rosette.*

FLOWERS *of one variety of* Aechmea chantinii *are bright red in color, borne on spikes.*

DEEP ORANGE *flowers tipped blue are followed by long-lasting berries—*Aechmea 'Royal Wine'.

VRIESIA 'Mariae'. Light green leaves are set off by flattened clusters of flowers encased in bracts.

THIS BILLBERGIA has long, arching spikes of flowers enclosed by bright red bracts.

ing flower stems. The blooms are followed by long-lasting berries.

A. 'Royal Wine': Dark green leaves backed with dark wine color. The flowers are deep orange tipped with blue.

Billbergia nutans: Green leaves with a silver cast beneath. Flowers borne on long, arching stems are chartreuse-green tipped in violet-blue with protruding golden stamens. The bracts are rose-red. The tubular flowers open one by one, and since there are 4-12 on a spike, the display lasts a long time. The leaf arrangement is of the rosette type.

Cryptanthus zonatus 'Zebrinus': Stiff, reddish bronze leaves marked with silver cross bands. White flowers in a small, nestlike cluster grow from the center of the plant. The plant has a flattish rosette of handsome leaves.

Dyckia fosteriana: Leaves of silvery gray, or occasionally reddish brown to bronze. Orange flowers in spikelike clusters appear on tall, slender stems. The plants grow best in full sun.

Guzmania lingulata: Rosettes of smooth metallic green leaves centered with bright red bracts; the inner bracts are orange-red tipped with white or shades of yellow. The white flowers are relatively

inconspicuous because the bracts are so showy. The plant is quite sensitive to frost and burns in direct sunlight.

Neoregelia carolinae 'Tricolor': Green and white striped leaves that turn pink (crimson near the center). The flowers are blue and are formed low in the cup in the center of the plant.

Nidularium innocentii: Straplike leaves with spiny margins. Brilliant red bractlike leaves make a smaller rosette at the center. From this rosette the flowers arise—a dense bunch of white flowers with erect petals. Several varieties are available.

Tillandsia ionantha: Leaves in the center of the plant turn bright red just before the small clusters of violet flowers begin to show. The plant grows to 4 inches in height.

Vriesia 'Mariae': Light green leaves. The yellow flowers rise in clusters above leaves and are encased in bracts that are red at the base and yellow dotted with brown at the tip.

V. splendens 'Major': Wide-spreading, dark green leaves banded with a deep reddish purple beneath, lighter on top. The long-lasting, 24-inch-long, flattened flower spike has yellowish white flowers sheathed in brilliant red bracts.

66 BROMELIADS

DYCKIA FOSTERIANA *forms dense rosettes of leaves with spine-toothed edges, sharp tips.*

AECHMEA 'ROYAL WINE'. *The undersides of the long, arching leaves are a deep wine color.*

TILLANDSIA IONANTHA *is a tufted plant with bristled, thick, narrow, pointed leaves.*

GUZMANIA LINGULATA *has a rosette of metallic green leaves around bright flower bracts.*

ORCHIDS

A touch of the exotic

You don't need a greenhouse to grow orchids. There are many varieties that are adaptable to growing in the home, and with a little understanding of their native growth habits, you will find they will flourish and bloom. Many of these plants can be transferred to the patio or garden for the summer.

Orchids come from all parts of the world. They can be found high in the mountains, up in the tops of trees refreshed by tropical breezes, beside streams, beneath waterfalls, and often in open meadows. The orchids that grow in trees or upon rocks are called epiphytes—that is, they are air plants deriving their nourishment from debris that collects in crooks of branches or in rock crevices and from moisture in the air. They are not parasites. These plants often have thickened leaves and stems to store water.

Other orchids grow on the ground and are called terrestrials. Their roots are always moist, though not soggy. The soil in which they grow drains rapidly so that the roots do not stand in water which would cause them to rot.

Obviously, orchids are quite different from other plants in their cultural needs and native habitat. That does not mean, however, that these plants are difficult or impossible to grow; they just require different care and understanding of their cultural needs.

COLLECTION of orchids displayed on pebble-filled tray. Cattleyas, phalaenopsis, and ferns are grown here near a window which is located next to the eating area.

MILTONIA, *pansy orchid, has flowers to 4 inches wide with many colors and markings.*

HERE *are* Cattleya *orchids (left),* Phalaenopsis *(upper right),* Paphiopedilum, Miltonia *(lower right).*

PHALAENOPSIS, *often called moth orchid, is usually white, pink, or speckled.*

PAPHIOPEDILUM *(often sold as* Cypripedium*) has waxy flowers to 8 inches wide, in many colors.*

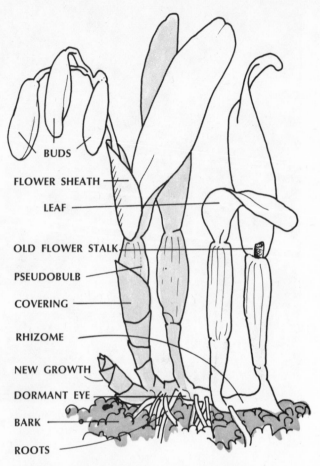

BUDS

FLOWER SHEATH

LEAF

OLD FLOWER STALK

PSEUDOBULB

COVERING

RHIZOME

NEW GROWTH

DORMANT EYE

BARK

ROOTS

SYMPODIAL TYPE of growth. Cattleya rhizome with pseudobulb, leaves, flowers growing up from it.

DECORATIVE USES FOR ORCHIDS

Orchids are not as attractive as many foliage plants when not blooming. The structure of the plants and the leaves is functional but not noted for its beauty. Orchids are best grown in an area where their cultural needs can be met. Then when the plants are in bloom (in some cases, such as *Phalaenopsis*, blooming continues for months) they can be placed in the house where the rare beauty of the flowers can be enjoyed. Orchids can be placed with other plants in an attractive arrangement, or singly on a table. There is no doubt that the lovely plants will provoke many comments and will be the source of a great deal of satisfaction to you.

CONTAINERS

Everyone who grows orchids, whether hobbyist or commercial grower, has his opinion about the best kind of container for the plants. There are several alternatives, and your choice should be based on personal preference as well as your own habits in the watering and care of your orchids.

Clay pots still seem to be the standard container. There are special orchid pots with slits up the sides, but the ordinary clay pot is quite adequate. The drainage hole may be enlarged somewhat to insure better drainage and aeration of the roots.

Plastic pots are gaining in popularity, and many growers prefer them. It has been found that the potting medium in plastic pots stays several degrees warmer than in clay. However, watering schedules must be adjusted to take into consideration the fact that these pots retain moisture much more effectively than clay does and won't need to be watered as frequently.

Many orchids can also be grown in baskets. Redwood construction with the pieces of wood fairly close together so that the potting medium will be well contained is the most desirable. Orchids look very attractive in this type of container.

Some orchids can also be grown on pieces of osmunda or tree fern. The material can be obtained in logs, poles, and slabs, and the plants may be either wired or stapled to them. Plants with cascading flower spikes can be very attractive on a slab that is hung so that the flowers cascade downward.

Wooden or plastic planters are very effective containers for cymbidiums. Some growers use large plastic pails, while others prefer redwood planters.

GROWTH CHARACTERISTICS

In general the structure of orchids is the same as that of other plants. They have roots, stems, leaves, and flowers. But orchids do differ in some respects.

There are two types of growth in orchid plants: sympodial and monopodial (see drawings, pages 70, 71). With sympodial growth, there is a creeping stem (rhizome) from which the roots go down and the leaves and flowers go up. The rhizome is woody, and the new growth originates from the apex, usually after flowering; generally there is only one new growth a year.

The stem that rises from the rhizome is called a pseudobulb and is much thickened. Though it is not a true bulb, it functions as one, storing water and food. The shape of the pseudobulb varies in different kinds of orchids.

Above the pseudobulb rise one to three leaves, depending upon the kind. The leaves are usually leathery and almost succulent in nature. Water loss is considerably cut down because of this fact.

There is a great variation in the size, color, and shape of the leaves. Some are straplike, while others are broad, and the color variation is wide. As the new pseudobulbs are formed, the leaves on the back bulbs turn yellow and fall off over a period of years. Gradually the pseudobulb withers and also turns yellow. When the plants are divided, this older portion is cut off and usually discarded.

The flower spikes arise from within the folds of the leaves and are enclosed by sheaths (protective coverings). One or many flowers can be borne on one spike. There is a wide and fascinating variation in the form and the color of the flowers.

The roots of the orchids grow down and out from the rhizome and are white in color and rather fleshy in nature. Some of the roots will not grow into the potting medium and will extend over the pot. Since these plants are not confined in nature, it is often difficult to domesticate them. The other roots weave in and out through the potting mix and absorb water and nutrients to sustain the plants. As the roots grow old, they turn brown and can be cut off when the plant is repotted.

The other form of growth is monopodial—a plant with only one stem that grows continuously upward. Sometimes the stem is visible, and in other cases it is covered by the leaves. As the plant grows upward, the older leaves at the bottom turn yellow and fall off.

In the monopodial type of growth, the plants do not produce pseudobulbs, so they do not have any water storage mechanism. Therefore, the potting medium must always be kept moist and not be allowed to dry out as the sympodials require. The medium must be porous and fast draining or the roots may rot and the plant die.

The roots are white and fleshy, similar to the sympodials, and may be pale green when wet. Again, the old roots are brown. Many aerial roots are produced along the stem. Some will go into the potting medium, while others will go over the pot's edge.

Flowers are produced in spikes from the leaf axils along the stem. More mature plants may produce several spikes each season. These plants do not produce a sheath. The flower spikes can bear many flowers and will usually arch over the plant.

GROWTH REQUIREMENTS

The cultural needs of orchids are different from those of other plants because of their structure and native growth habits. These needs are discussed in the section that follows. Remember, orchids can stand a great deal of neglect, if this neglect is tempered with understanding.

Temperature: Orchids fall naturally into three distinct groups by virtue of their temperature requirements—warm-growing (night temperature near 70°, day near 80°), intermediate (night temperature

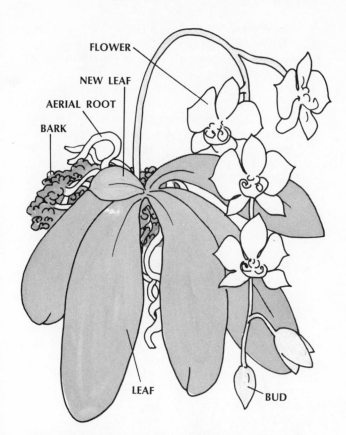

MONOPODIAL TYPE *of growth. In this drawing a phalaenopsis plant represents growth habit.*

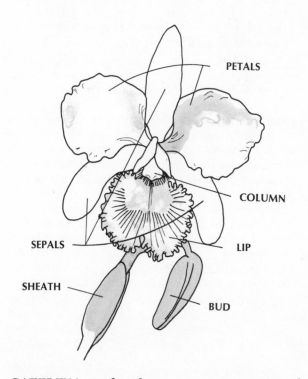

CATTLEYA *in this drawing is representative of orchid flower structure.*

around 60°, day 70°-75°), and cool (night temperature 50°-55°, day 65°-70°). The drop in the night temperature is important, for it slows down transpiration and therefore speeds up growth. The cooler nights have also been found necessary in some cases to set the flower buds.

No hard and fast rules can be made for keeping plants in their temperature range. It has been found that many, though not all, orchids from different groups can be combined and grown well in the same room. It is essential that you know what the temperature range is in the area where you wish to grow the plants and then obtain plants that will grow well there. Some modifications can be made for providing minor variations within the same room. For example, the warm-growing orchids could be placed nearer the source of heat than the intermediate ones. A little experience and watching for signs from your plants will soon teach you whether your plants are happy or not.

Light: Here again there is a wide variation in requirements. A good rule to follow is to give your plants all the sun they can take without burning. A lush green plant may look nice but probably will not bloom. Most healthy orchid plants are a light green in color. Brown spots on the leaves and pseudobulbs indicate too much sun.

Morning sun is most beneficial, so locate your plants where they will receive as much morning sun as possible. Artificial lights have proved to be very satisfactory for orchids. Using this means of light, plants can be grown in dark areas, garages, and even basements. (See the chapter on Fluorescent Light Gardening, pages 84-89.)

Water: The amount of water and frequency of watering are the most critical factors in successful orchid growing. If in doubt as to whether to water your plants, *don't*. When to water depends upon the plant type, size of pot, potting medium, and humidity. A little experience will teach you when to water and how often. Tap the pot; if it sounds hollow, it is dry. Or feel the outside of a clay pot; if it is warm, it needs water. A finger poked down into the potting medium is also a good test.

When you water, do it well. Let water run through the potting medium, and then soak it again. Then allow the plant to dry out. Types with the monopodial habit of growth always need to be moist, but never soggy. These plants do not have water storage structures so need constant moisture at the roots.

If you have many plants, it will be helpful and time saving to group like kinds together, with seedlings in small pots in a group. In this way, those of like needs can be taken care of in less time.

Humidity: This is the amount of moisture in the air. Achieving the required humidity for orchids can prove a little difficult in the house. However, there

BEFORE. *This cattleya orchid has outgrown its container, needs to be divided, repotted.*

are a number of things you can do to raise the humidity. Spraying the plants daily with a fine mist will be beneficial—but do not let the plants go into the night wet, as wet leaves could promote disease and pest infestations.

Another good solution is to place the pots in trays that have been filled with stones. The trays can then be filled with water to a level just below the tops of the stones. The bottoms of the pots should not be sitting in the water. A relative humidity of 40-60 per cent is desirable, but the plants can do well with lower humidity.

Ventilation: As orchids in nature are constantly refreshed by fresh, moving air, this is also an essential ingredient in the home culture of these plants. Orchids will not thrive in stagnant, unmoving air. In providing for ventilation, avoid drafts directly on the plants.

Fertilizing: Most orchid growers sell special fertilizer for orchids, and the directions for use will be included. Read these carefully and follow them for best results.

The type of potting medium you use will dictate the amount and kind of fertilizer that you use. Osmunda needs little or no fertilizer, while fir bark has no nutrients and needs a regular program. Current trends indicate success with frequent applications of fertilizer that has been diluted to half or less of full strength.

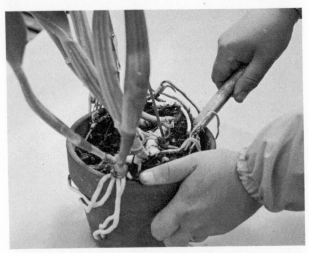

1. CAREFULLY *pry plant out of pot with tapered, blunt tool. Don't pull out by stems. Hold pot firmly.*

2. NEXT, *work all of old bark chunks from roots with your fingers, being careful to avoid root damage.*

3. CUT *rhizome with sharp pruning shears. Remove withered stems; leave 3 or 4 stems per division.*

4. TRIM *off all dead roots, saving as many healthy roots as possible. Shorten extra long ones.*

5. INSPECT *plants for signs of disease. Discard unhealthy plants, dust cuts with sulfur or ferbam.*

6. PLACE *rhizome so cut end is against edge of pot with growth bud about in center of pot.*

Sequence continued on page 74.

Sequence continued from page 73.

7. *POUR bark into pot. Tap pot gently to settle bark around roots. Leave ½ inch space at top.*

8. *SET stake firmly in bark and tie each stem with string so leaves are upright.*

9. *LABEL plants. Wet bark and pot with thorough watering, fertilize when new growth starts.*

Pests, diseases, and control: Orchids are subject to scale, mealybugs, aphids, thrips, beetles, weevils, and slugs and snails. The best procedure is to prevent infestations; be neat and clean—wash plants regularly and inspect for any insects. There are a number of diseases to which orchids are subject, and the topic can be complex. If you purchase your plants from a reputable grower, you should not have any problem with orchid diseases. (See chapter on Pests and Diseases, pages 81-83.)

PROPAGATION

Most sympodial orchids can be propagated by division. When they outgrow their pots, healthy plants can be divided in two. (See photographs and instructions, pages 73, 74.) Plants are grown commercially from seed in flasks containing agar and nutrients; they can be grown in this manner by amateur growers, but it is a complex field and cannot be discussed in detail here. (In general, a period of seven years is required from seed to a blooming plant.)

Seedlings can be purchased from growers at a low cost and can provide an inexpensive way to increase your collection. However, when first embarking on growing orchids, choose mature blooming plants. That way you know what you are getting and can enjoy the plant in bloom from the inception of your interest.

POTTING MIXES FOR ORCHIDS

MATURE CATTLEYAS, PHALAENOPSIS, ETC.

$\frac{1}{8}$"-$\frac{5}{8}$" fir bark

Seedlings $\frac{1}{4}$"-$\frac{1}{2}$"
or
Osmunda or true fern

CYPRIPEDIUMS

Osmunda or cymbidium mix

CYMBIDIUMS

8 parts fir bark $\frac{1}{4}$"-$\frac{5}{8}$"

2 parts dry oak leaves

Note: Potting mixes and bark of different kinds and sizes are all readily available. It is simpler and more reliable to use these. The suggested formulas above may be varied to suit your own needs.

POTTING AND REPOTTING

The repotting of a mature cattleya has been shown in a sequence of photographs, pages 73, 74. This method applies in general to all orchids, whether sympodial or monopodial.

It is time to repot when the orchid has outgrown its pot or when the potting medium has become decomposed. This usually occurs every two or three years. It is best to repot orchids just after they bloom, at which time the plants are putting out new roots.

When using osmunda, the medium must be packed tightly around the roots; a stick works well for doing this. After the plant has been potted, trim off the pieces of osmunda that protrude above the top edge of the pot.

ENCYCLOPEDIA

The list that follows is not meant to be a complete list of the kinds of orchids that you can grow in the house. Rather, the plants listed are intended as suggestions and have proven to be very satisfactory as house plants. You can go on from here.

Angraecum sesquipedale: Long-stalked, waxy, ivory white flowers and 12 to 18-inch-long spur. Flowers are quite fragrant at night. Bloom is in December.

Cattleya: A large genus of the orchid family which includes the large, showy, and familiar corsage orchid. The genus has become larger because of the adaptability of these plants to being crossed both between themselves and with other kinds of orchids. A wealth of colors and forms is available.

A minimum of 55° night temperature is advisable, although these plants can endure a few colder nights. A daytime rise of 10°-15° is required. In the summer the plants can be cooled somewhat by frequent misting. Cattleyas require a great deal of light to flower, so don't be afraid to give it to them.

Coelogyne: Includes easy-to-grow and readily available species *C. cristata*. It has pendulous white flowers with yellow throats. They are produced in profusion, up to 10 fragrant blooms to a stem. Flowers measure 2-3 inches across. Plants do best when crowded in the pot. Osmunda is a good potting medium.

Cymbidium: Includes two forms—the large type and the miniature (see photographs on this page). These orchids need cool weather to set blossoms and can be grown outdoors in mild-winter areas. Light frost will not be harmful if the plants are in a protected area.

Cymbidiums need good light; here again, give them all they can take without burning. They prefer

COMPARISON *of flowers of large and miniature cymbidiums. The scale is one inch per grid division.*

BRING *miniature cymbidiums in when they are blooming. This one provides accent on an end table.*

a night temperature of 45°-55° and as much as 80° or 90° during the day.

Cypripedium: See *Paphiopedilum*

Epidendrum: Those with pseudobulbs may be grown with cattleyas; reed-stemmed types are garden plants in warmer climates. Flower sizes and shapes vary, and there are many generic crosses in which epidendrums are used.

Laelia: Grows most satisfactorily on slabs. The plants have the characteristic cattleya-type foliage and flowers. Blooms are produced on long, arching stems and open in succession, prolonging the bloom period for the already long-lasting flowers to a month or more. Among the species easiest to grow and most readily available are the following:

L. anceps, autumn and winter blooming, violet-rose with yellow throat lined with purple; *L. albida,* winter and early spring flowering, white with yellow ribs in the throat; *L. autumnalis,* late autumn and winter blooming (needs good chilling to flower), rose-purple with white at the base of the lip.

ODONTOGLOSSUM (upper left), Laelia *(upper right),* Paphiopedilum *(lower left),* Miltonia.

Other readily available, easy-to-grow varieties include *L. furfuracea,* which produces pink flowers in October. These may be 3-5 inches across, and each stem carries one to three flowers. *L. gouldiana* resembles *L. autumnalis,* but its flowers are deep rosy purple; leaves may show purple tinting in strong sun. *L. speciosa (L. grandiflora)* has long-lasting flowers that may reach 6 inches in breadth. Old plants have an odd look, with many of the older growths leafless; leaves and flowers are concentrated at the growing tips. To bloom well it needs full sun and some drying off in winter.

Miltonia warscewiczii: Flowers 2 inches wide with wavy sepals and petals, both reddish brown tipped with yellow. Lip is yellow in the center, bordered with white, and has rose-purple blotches. Up to 40 of these blooms may appear in each 2-foot-long branched flower cluster. Bloom is in December.

Odontoglossum: Kinds well adapted to container culture are those native to high altitudes, where they are continually moistened by fog and cold rain. Use finely chopped osmunda fiber or ground bark as a potting mix. Transplant the orchids after they have flowered. Don't overpot them; they thrive when crowded. They thrive under the same conditions as do cymbidiums but will be damaged by frost. *O. grande* has 4-inch-wide flowers, bright yellow with mahogany brown stripes, giving it the name tiger orchid. Other easy-to-grow species include *O. bictoniense,* which has pink flowers on stiff stems above light green foliage and is hardy to about 22°, and *O. pulchellum,* the lily-of-the-valley orchid, which produces six or more fragrant white flowers on a 10-inch stem.

Oncidium: Readily damaged by frost, although a number of the oncidiums are cool-growing orchids. It is best to winter these plants inside and move them out when the weather is warmer. Shade them from the hot afternoon sun. Plant them in osmunda fiber or coarsely ground bark, or wire them to a slab so the pendulous flower spray can hang down. Give them an abundance of water during the growing season, but withhold water for 2 to 3 weeks after growth matures to insure good flower formation.

The hardiest of this group is *O. cavendishianum,* with thick broad leaves and bright yellow, 2-inch-wide flower stems. Other good ones are *O. splendidum,* with tall sprays of 2-inch-wide flowers marked reddish brown on yellow-green background, and *O. tigrinum,* having large yellow flowers with wide chocolate brown stripes and a yellow lip.

Paphiopedilum (often called *Cypripedium*): Name which is now applied to the lady slipper orchids native to the Old World tropics. In this group, probably the easiest to grow is *P. insigne.* It has graceful, arching, straplike leaves and polished

ONCIDIUM *(top left)*, Stanhopea *(right)*, Angraecum *(bottom left)*, Zygopetalum *(right)*.

CORNER *of a living room bookshelf makes pleasant setting for* Paphiopedilum *and palm.*

FLOWERS *of lady slipper orchids may be white, yellow, green with white stripes, all green, or a combination of background colors and markings in tan, mahogony, brown, maroon, green, or white.*

ORCHIDS *make delightful gifts and can be shipped almost anywhere in bud or flower.*

lady-slipper-type blooms on stiff, brown, hairy stems. It blooms any time from October to March. Color range: Sepals and petals are green and white, spotted and striped brown; the pouch is reddish brown.

P. insigne is hardy to about 28° for short periods of time. Grow these lady slippers in pots, using a potting medium of equal parts finely chopped osmunda fiber or ground bark and sandy loam.

Phalaenopsis: Lovely warm-growing orchids especially adaptable for culture in the house. The temperature range should be between 65° and 85°. There are many species and hybrids from which to choose as well as a wide range of colors—yellow, white, pink (some with stripes). The flowers are borne on long, arching sprays that are very lovely and long-lasting. More mature plants will send out several spikes simultaneously. They bloom in late winter and spring. Under the proper conditions phalaenopsis will bloom twice yearly. Plant them in any standard orchid potting mix; they do well in bark. These plants must be kept moist but well drained. Fresh, moving air is essential.

Stanhopea tigrina: Flower stems about a foot long, growing down through potting medium and producing four to six waxy and fragrant 5 to 6-inch-wide blooms, buff yellow with maroon markings. Bloom may be any time of the year.

Zygopetalum mackayi: Five to seven very fragrant blooms, 2¾-4 inches wide, in 18 to 24-inch-long flower clusters. Sepals and petals are green with large, merging patches of brown. Lip, narrow at base, is bluish white with radiating purplish blue lines. Bloom is in the fall.

LACY *Boston fern complements a lovely golden phalaenopsis on a dining room buffet.*

LAZY-SUSAN *plant stand for display of orchids outdoors in mild weather. Stand holds 21 pots.*

TABLE surface serves to mirror a lovely white phalaenopsis with a pale pink lip. Most all orchids serve as dramatic centerpieces for dinner parties or just to enjoy daily.

MATURE flowering cattleya displays the familiar corsage orchids of the florist's shop.

HANGING baskets provide additional display space for orchids, especially cascading types, here vandas.

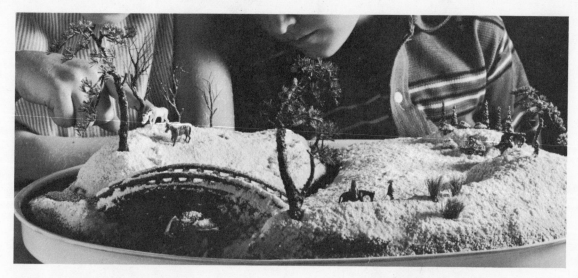

CHILDREN gently move horses in snow scene. "Snow" can be freshened or replaced.

JAPANESE MINIATURE LANDSCAPES

You'll find hours of enjoyment in creating a Japanese miniature landscape, and at the same time you'll sharpen your appreciation of Oriental design. The Japanese have developed several kinds of miniature scenes: bonsai, bonkei, saikei, bonseki, suiseki. The materials vary somewhat in the different scenes; some use only artificial materials, while others make use of live plants.

The thought that should dominate in the creation of a tray landscape is that nature must be imitated on a very small scale. Visualize a favorite scene or find a photograph of one that appeals to you and then proceed to duplicate it as closely as possible. Keep the scene simple, for in this quality lies the beauty of miniature landscapes.

Materials: The container should be a shallow, attractive bowl or tray. Drainage is essential, so if your container does not have a hole, it would be best to drill one. The color and texture of the container should be in keeping with the mood of your scene. The container should aid in creating the atmosphere but not be obtrusive.

The plants must be selected with care and an eye to the final effect that you desire. Trees with small leaves, flowers, and fruits are desirable to maintain balance. Young seedling trees are very suitable.

If rocks or pebbles are to be used, select those that will follow the lines you wish to form. A great deal of enjoyment can come from selecting the materials for your landscape, and this selection will dictate the final product. Choose with care— time and patience will be rewarded.

The potting soil can be of your own choice, or you can use the following mix: ⅓ sand, ⅓ leaf mold or peat moss, ⅓ earth. A faster draining soil can be made by changing these proportions to include more sand.

The surface of the landscape may be sand sprinkled on the top of the soil, or grass or moss may be planted. Small figurines, animals, or huts can be added for variety or to set the theme. Here again, be sparing in their use.

Planting: Place a piece of broken pot over the drainage hole in the bottom of the tray or container. Place a small amount of the potting mix on the bottom. Trim the long, straggly roots of the trees, except in the case of pines. Next, set the trees and rocks in the positions you desire. Moisten the soil so that it will hold its shape when pressed into a ball in your hand. This will keep the trees in place. Plant the trees. Build up hills, carve out valleys for streams or hollows for lakes or ponds. Finish off by planting moss or grass or covering with sand.

Care: Your miniature landscape should receive some sun, preferably morning sun, and should be protected from drying winds. Miniature landscapes can be kept in the house for short periods to be enjoyed close at hand, and then they can be refreshed by being returned outdoors.

Water the plants when they are dry. Do not allow long periods without water. Space should be allowed for air to circulate around the plants. Do not crowd containers together. If you have created several landscapes, a special display area can be constructed to display them.

PESTS AND DISEASES

If you find signs of insects, consult the chart on the next two pages

House plants are less susceptible to disease and infestations than are plants in a greenhouse or garden. Taking simple precautions that have been noted previously in this book can reduce the chances of infestation even more, so it seems worthwhile to note them again.

1. Always use clean pots and sterilized soil to prevent infestations by soil pests.

2. Examine new plants and cut flowers that you are bringing into the house for the first time to be certain they are free of pests.

3. Isolate new potted plants for a month and inspect frequently for signs of disease or insects.

4. Wash leaves of plants with lukewarm water to which a small amount of mild detergent has been added. The removal of dust will improve the appearance of the plants.

5. Remove any dead leaves and inspect plants frequently for signs of poor health.

6. If insects are found, take action immediately. One infested plant can be handpicked, washed, and isolated. If the infestation is on a larger scale, refer to the chart on pages 82-83 and treat. Take action quickly.

Read the directions on labels carefully and follow them exactly. Be certain the spray is safe for plants. It is best to use insecticides outdoors if possible. The pushbutton spray cans are convenient and save the trouble of mixing sprays. They are easy to use and economical when only a few plants need to be sprayed. Follow label directions. When the spray is not in use, keep it covered tightly and out of the reach of children.

House plants are not as subject to disease as are greenhouse plants. If you buy healthy plants from a reputable source, you should not have any disease problem. Crown or root rot may occur, but it is likely to be caused by poor drainage and overwatering. Loss of leaves and spotting may be caused by low humidity. Once the situation is corrected the problem should not exist.

The same basic principles of gardening apply to plants in the house as to those in the garden. It is always easier to take precautionary measures. A little time spent keeping plants clean will be a good long-term investment.

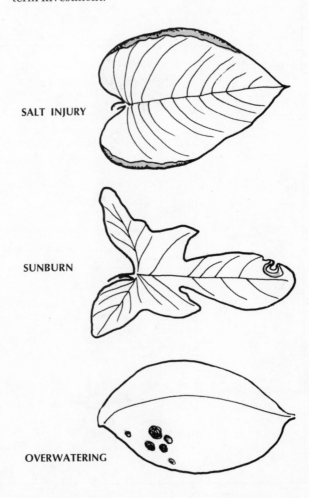

SALT INJURY

SUNBURN

OVERWATERING

PESTS AND CONTROL

NAME	DESCRIPTION	DAMAGE	CONTROL
ANTS	Black, brown, or red. They live in nests or colonies, are attracted to plants by certain aphids, mealybugs, and scale insects which excrete honeydew.	Ants can carry away seeds or seedlings and may injure roots.	Soak infested soil, pots, and boxes with malathion or diazinon.
APHIDS	Sucking insects with soft, round or pear-shaped bodies—many colors and kinds. They usually cluster on new growth and buds.	Aphids suck plant juices, causing poor growth, stunted plants, or curled, distorted leaves. They secrete a sticky liquid called honeydew, which provides a base for the growth of sooty mold.	Dip or spray plants, using malathion, diazinon, or a systemic insecticide.
MEALYBUGS	Soft-bodied sucking insects that appear as if they had been dusted with powder. Visible to the eye, they cluster in leaf axils or branch crotches.	They secrete honeydew on which black mold grows. Sucking of mealybugs stunts or kills plants.	If only one plant is infested, isolate it and handpick or touch with cotton swab dipped in alcohol. Otherwise dip or spray plants with malathion, being certain to wet mealybugs thoroughly. Use a pressure spray.
MITES, CYCLAMEN	Too small to be visible, but when magnified are seen to be oval, semi-transparent. They attack tender young leaves and buds.	Leaves become twisted; buds are deformed. Blackening of infested parts is common. The mites crawl from plant to plant where leaves touch and can be transferred on hands or clothing.	Isolate plant immediately. Dip or spray, using a systemic insecticide as directed on the label. Trim off infested parts of plant where practicable.

MITES, SPIDER	Cannot be seen unless there are many together. Flat, oval, usually red. Found on undersides of leaves.	Leaves may yellow and die, or drop off. Infected plants become stunted and may die.	Spray or dip plants, using a systemic insecticide or diazinon. Be certain to wet the underside of the foliage.
SCALES	Many kinds. Some have a shell-like covering or scale that covers the entire body. Browns and grays are the predominant colors. Some kinds attack leaves, others stems, some both.	Scales are sucking insects that use plant juices for food. The result is a stunted plant or one that grows poorly. Scales also secrete honeydew which attracts ants.	Spray or dip, using malathion. Repeat as directed on label. If only one or two plants are infested, washing is an effective control method.
THRIPS	Very small, barely visible. They are slender and colored tan, brown, brownish black, or black with lighter markings. Young are whitish to yellow or orange. Some species carry droplets of black excrement on their backs. Adults fly or leap when plant is disturbed.	Thrips cause injury on plant or flowers by rasping the plant tissues and obtaining the juices. This rasping damage is often visible. Injury appears as distortion of leaves and flowers.	Dip or spray plants, using malathion, diazinon, or a systemic insecticide.
WHITEFLIES	Very small, common pests with white, wedge-shaped wings. They flutter about when plant is disturbed, resembling small snowflakes. Young attach to undersurfaces of leaves.	Whiteflies feed on plant juices, turning leaves pale. Surfaces of leaves become covered with excreted honeydew, and sooty mold may develop.	Dip or spray plants, using diazinon or malathion. Several applications may be needed—follow label directions.

FLUORESCENT LIGHT GARDENING

You can increase your growing area by the use of artificial lights

Lacking a good outside source of light or having utilized all of the available light, you can still have a thriving collection of house plants if you use artificial light to illuminate the growing area you have set aside for your plants. This area can be anywhere in the house—an unused book shelf, a room divider planter, part of the garage, a basement, a space over the kitchen counter—any spot that would be improved by the addition of growing plants.

Plants respond best to the artificial light that most closely approximates sunlight. In natural sunlight, plants use chiefly the red and blue radiant energy from the opposite ends of the spectrum—about twice as much red light as blue light. Red light stimulates vegetative growth; blue light regulates the respiratory system.

One of the best ways to provide the essential light for plant growth is to use a combination of ordinary fluorescent lights—daylight and natural are the best. Incandescent lights, generally, are not strong enough in the red or blue color bands, generate too much heat for tender plant leaves, and deliver only about a third as much light for the same amount of electricity as do fluorescent lights. The addition of incandescent lights to fluorescent lights was at one time felt to be essential. There are some growers who still feel that using an incandescent bulb of low wattage does aid plant growth. It is not, however, necessary.

Several manufacturers of electric lights and fixtures have developed fluorescent tubes designed especially for growing plants indoors. Each tube combines a high intensity of light at both the red and blue ends of the spectrum. Some growers use these tubes exclusively, while others use them in combination with the standard fluorescent tubes.

The special tubes are available in standard fluorescent lamp sizes from 24 inches to 96 inches and will fit into ordinary fluorescent fixtures. They emit a pale lavender light—an important point to keep in mind if you keep an indoor plant collection in a prominent place where colors might clash. You can design your own combination light stand and planter or install fixtures over existing planters.

PLANTERS AND FIXTURES

There are planters on the market that incorporate fixtures to accommodate either standard fluorescent lights or the special plant lights. You can buy either hanging basket units or standing units for a table top or planter. Before purchasing any unit, take careful measurement to be certain that the space you have set aside will be large enough to accommodate the fixture that you intend to place there. These units tend to be somewhat expensive, so if you have a limited amount of money to spend, it would be more economical to improvise your own.

Used fluorescent light fixtures may be purchased in many areas. Watch the want ads for such items. Often these fixtures are removed from office buildings that are being remodeled and are sold at a modest cost. If there will be no surface directly above the fixture, buy a unit with a reflector or make one out of aluminum that can be purchased at hardware stores. Buy a fixture that will fit in the space in which you intend to use it. As a general rule, allow 15-20 watts of light per square foot of growing area. One large unit is better than two small ones, for the light output is lower at the ends of the tubes. The fixtures that take two or four tubes are best. One tube is really not enough to grow plants.

If the lights are to be placed over an existing planter, the plants are already taken care of. If, however, you are placing plants in a new location, a planter will have to be constructed. A simple box can be made and lined with heavy plastic. Over the plas-

TABLE-TOP FIXTURE designed for growing African violets, seedlings, begonias. This one contains one growth lamp, one cool white fluorescent lamp. Many plants could be grown in this manner.

tic a layer of stones, sand, or vermiculite can be placed to provide a drip tray and to raise the humidity. The material should be kept moist. Place the potted plants directly on the stones, but do not allow them to sit in water. Be certain that your planter is watertight so that no water will leak out to stain floors, carpets, or shelves.

The lifetime of the tubes varies according to their use. The number of times that the lights are turned on and off will also affect their life span. It is a good practice to replace the tubes every six months or so in order to have the maximum output from them. Black rings will form at the ends of regular fluorescent tubes—this is an indication that the tubes should be replaced. Buy preheat tubes rather than rapid start as their life will be longer and they are somewhat less expensive. The ballasts will sometimes have to be replaced on either.

It is helpful to install an automatic timer to turn the lights on and off on a regular schedule. These timers are not very expensive and will save you enough effort in the long run to be worth the cost.

For best results, expose most plants to about 12 hours of artificial light a day. Some plants' requirements will vary somewhat from this mean; you will have to experiment to determine the exact length of artificial daylight that is best. Some plants can take, and thrive on, 16 hours of light a day, while others,

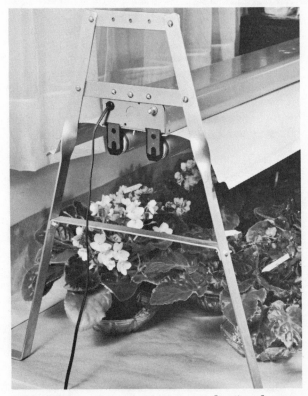

SIDE VIEW of stand. Frame of 1 by ⅛-inch strap iron holds 48-inch industrial fluorescent fixture.

BASEMENT *garden room constructed for the growing of plants. The only light is artificial.*

THREE-TIERED *plant stand for growing African violets. Lamps are turned on 14 hours a day.*

MANUFACTURED *table-top unit with adjustable brass enamel reflector. Units come in various sizes.*

such as orchids, will not flower if given that much light.

Place the lights about 6 to 8 inches above the soil surface if you are growing seedlings in flats, about 12 to 15 inches above the foliage of mature plants in pots. If you are constructing your own light setup, the fixtures can be placed on chains so that they can be easily raised and lowered. If the fixtures are on a permanent stand or attached to the wall, the plants can be raised by placing them on pots of varying heights. If the plants become leggy, they are not receiving enough light. If the foliage is bunched together unnaturally, they are receiving too much light.

Plants that are grown under lights need a regular feeding schedule. Since foliar growth and root production are kept at a constant level, the plants must be continually supplied with food. A humidity of about 50 per cent is desirable; night temperature should be about 10 degrees less than that of the daytime (about 62° night temperature, 72° day).

Most kinds of plants thrive under fluorescent lights. Experience has shown that orchids, African violets, begonias, and foliage plants will grow and flower there. Try any plant for a period of time and see how it will grow. The scope of gardening under lights really has no bounds. Seeds, seedlings, and cuttings can be brought into full growth and flower much more quickly under lights than on windowsills because the source of light is constant.

It is also possible to grow plants under lights in an area removed from the living region of the home. Then when they are in flower they may be displayed under a light setup in the living area. When bloom is finished or new plants are ready to be displayed, the plants may be taken back to the growing area.

Fluorescent light gardening is adaptable for commercial establishments, where light is often not as good as it should be. The growth tubes impart a lush glow to the plants, making everything look very attractive.

Because lights are used in aquariums, a section follows on the planting of aquariums. The special growth tubes are manufactured in sizes to fit aquariums. In addition to aiding growth of marine plants, the lavender light brings out brilliant hues in such fish as veiltail guppies and swordtails. Reflector units that contain the light fixtures are made to fit all standard-sized tanks.

PLANTING AN AQUARIUM

Planting an aquarium is as important as arranging flowers decoratively in a bowl on the table—and for similar reasons. Contrary to general belief, plants really aren't needed in an aquarium except to enhance its beauty. Fish can be just as healthy in a tank that contains no plants at all. When the right plants are added, however, they reduce chances of excessive growth of algae and provide food and a hiding place for fish, a resting place for eggs and young, and a more natural habitat for the aquarium tenants.

Most aquarium owners agree that the plants are more difficult to raise than the fish, and if you have gardening experience you know this could be true. Requirements vary, and an aquarium is an unnatural environment. Nevertheless, with care you can grow healthy and handsome plants. The principal rule is to begin with samples of several kinds of plants, then buy more of those that do well in your particular combination of light, water, and fish. The light can be adjusted, and the water conditions can be adjusted to some extent; but certain fish eat certain plants, and some fish eat all plants.

Generally, aquatic plants are sold in three categories: rooted, bunch, and floating plants. Both rooted and bunch plants will thrive in just a couple of inches of very coarse sand. Droppings from the fish provide nutrients for them. Rooted plants can also be grown in soil, but when soil is used it should be contained in a pot and covered with sand so that it won't cloud the water.

Rooted Plants

These develop new growth from the center of a crown of leaves. Plant them the way you would perennials that grow in a similar manner—with the crowns resting on or just above the surface of the planting medium. These plants have long roots when you purchase them and should be planted individually with the roots completely covered.

All the rooted plants listed here are warm-water plants and should be limited to the tropical aquarium.

Water sprite (*Ceratopteris thalictroides*): May be classed as both a rooting and a floating plant. As it grows to the surface, new plants develop from buds which arise from all parts of the leaves, and the portion planted in the bottom of the aquarium dies off. It grows rapidly where it receives good light.

Cryptocoryne cordata: A shallow aquarium plant that does best where light is limited and where the light source is primarily from overhead rather than from the side. It prefers slightly acid water. Leaves are lance-shaped, olive green above, reddish purple beneath. Plants multiply by sending out runners with new crowns at the end. Several other small species of cryptocoryne are also available from shops specializing in aquaria and aquarium supplies.

Amazon sword plant (*Echinodorus intermedius*): Once a rarity but now becoming more generally available, although it is still considerably more expensive than the majority of aquarium plants. Leaves are oblong or lance-shaped, with 30 or 40 arising from a central crown. Plants reproduce by runners. The leaves are quite delicate and very vulnerable to damage by plant-eating snails. Amazon sword plant requires 8-10 hours of light a day. If other than the outer leaves turn brown, insufficient light is probably responsible; if algae grow on the surface of the leaves, the plants are receiving too much light.

Arrowhead (*Sagittaria natans*): A favorite among aquarium owners. Its 8-inch-long, grasslike foliage grows luxuriantly in an aquarium filled with clean, clear water and well stocked with fish. It requires plenty of light. Other species include S. *subulata*, a narrower and much thicker-leafed form, and S. *gigantea*, with half-inch-wide leaves to 2 feet long, for large aquariums. Often an aquarium is planted exclusively with sagittarias, with the taller growing species in the background and the smaller species in front.

Eel or tape grass (*Vallisneria spiralis*): Narrow undulating or spiral leaves arising from a central crown. It spreads by runners. It grows best in a well lighted aquarium, shaded from very strong light.

Bunch Plants

Aquarium stores classify unrooted cuttings of certain water plants as bunch plants. They used to be sold in large bunches held together with a lead ring, but since the lead cut into the stems, this method of packaging is being abandoned. When you buy these cuttings, strip the leaves from the basal inch of each stem and plant the ends about an inch deep in the sand. Group them in clumps in the aquarium. They will root quickly and grow rapidly.

Those listed here are cold-water plants, ideal for aquariums stocked with goldfish or guppies.

ANGELS, TIGERBARBS, SWORDTAILS swim in 60-gallon tank planted with water sprite, cryptocoryne. Plants make the tank attractive and more habitable for fish.

Elodea *(Anacharis canadensis):* Soft-stemmed plant with overlapping or whorled ½-inch leaves, requires 6-8 hours of strong light a day; it becomes stringy and leggy when light is insufficient. Select only crisp, dark-green-leafed cuttings for planting. Fish enjoy eating the leaves, but this plant grows so rapidly that you'll seldom notice they have touched it.

Fanwort *(Cabomba caroliniana):* Roots quickly and may grow 2-3 feet long, but it needs 8 hours of strong light each day. The submerged leaves are finely divided into hairlike segments; the floating leaves are undivided. Fanwort makes an excellent environment for spawning fish, both for the laying of eggs and for the hiding of young.

Hornwort *(Ceratophyllum demersum):* Another very fine-leafed plant that serves spawning fish well. It grows well in hard water and in poor light conditions. At times it gives off an unpleasant odor, which may rule it out for the home aquarium.

Floating Plants

These just float on the surface of the water and have no connecting link with the sand below. Their presence breaks up the smooth water surface, creating additional surface area for the escape of carbon dioxide, which tends to build up in a crowded aquarium and can suffocate the fish.

Azolla *(A. caroliana):* A small plant with divided greenish or reddish leaflike stems and tiny leaves. Azolla plants float in masses on the surface of the water.

Crystalwort *(Riccia fluitans):* A liverwort, closely related to the mosses. It is a bright green plant of attractive snowflake pattern, and it floats in masses just below the surface of the water. Newly hatched fish like to hide in it; some tropical fish lay their eggs in it.

Hygrophila polysperma: Most attractive planted in bunches in strong light. Hygrophila produces pairs of oblong leaves from a central stem and will grow to the surface of most home tanks.

Synnema triflorum: Sold as water wisteria, a fast grower under strong light. It has large, deeply lobed and cut leaves. The plants send out suckers that can be cut and rooted elsewhere.

Choosing a Tank

The best tank for tropical fish is the frame aquarium: a rectangular frame of stainless steel, with sides of good quality glass. Non-magnetic stainless steel, a nickel alloy, is more resistant to rust than is other stainless steel.

Aquariums can be purchased in standard sizes from 5-35 gallons. You pay proportionately more for the larger aquariums because the weight of water requires thicker glass and a stronger frame, and the deeper water necessitates a more efficient lighting system. Large aquariums may need a special support, as a cubic foot of water—7.7 gallons—weighs 62.3 pounds. Stands made of cast-iron can be purchased.

The tank should be nearly as wide as it is deep, for maximum natural aeration of the water. In such a tank, you can keep two or three small fish per gallon of water. If you are a beginner, you can hold down expense and trouble by limiting yourself to a tank of 10-15 gallons. It holds a satisfying number of fish (25-40) and is easy to keep at a constant temperature.

Heat

Tropical fish generally need a minimum temperature of 70°-75°; for some species the minimum is even higher. There are various thermostat-heater combinations. You will need a thermometer as well. Adjust thermostat to thermometer when the lights in the tank have been off for the night. Lights add extra heat.

When deciding on heater wattage, figure at the ratio of 5 watts per gallon. A 10-gallon tank will need a 50-watt heater.

Filtering and Aeration

Warm-water tanks require no connection to a water supply. But an air pump is necessary to provide both aeration and water circulation. Vibrator air pumps can be purchased that are not expensive.

A filter is an important part of the pumping system. One type stands inside the aquarium or hangs outside and uses charcoal and glass or nylon wool to remove both dirt and excessive gases. Another type is buried at the bottom of the aquarium and draws dirt down into the sand. You have to siphon the tank bottom regularly to remove dirt, unless there are very few fish. Plant roots may be damaged if an under-sand filter is run too fast; but the filter is invisible, so this choice is aesthetically more pleasing.

Whatever system you choose, be sure to buy an air-escape valve to insert between pump and filter. Most pumps produce too much air for a single filter, and some must be bled through the valve.

Lights

Light units especially designed for the various aquarium sizes can be purchased at aquarium stores. There are two types: those using regular incandescent bulbs and those using fluorescent bulbs.

Special bulbs for these fixtures are now available to promote more growth in the plants and intensify the brilliant colors of the fish.

The Fish

There is almost unlimited choice of size, shape, and color among tropical fish. Before actually buying fish, you should set up your aquarium, plant it, and allow the water to age and the plants to root. If there is any chlorine in your tap water, it will kill the fish; but after a day or two it escapes into the air. (For this reason, fresh additions of water should always be aged for at least a day.)

If this is your first venture into the realm of aquarium culture, it would be best to start with a few fish recommended by your local aquarium supplier. Then as you gain experience you can branch out to tropical fish more difficult to raise. Maintenance of tanks is not time consuming once the tanks are set up. You will find the pastime of fish watching quite enjoyable, and the picture presented by a well planted aquarium is a pleasure to the eye.

AQUARIUM dominates entry, screens dining area beyond without blocking view or light.

There is an appeal for all ages in a terrarium. For a child, a terrarium is a miniature garden that he can watch grow and change. For an adult, it can be an incubator to give house plants as good a start as they would get in a greenhouse. It is especially attractive at night when the plants can be lighted from above and imparted with a soft glow.

Terrariums can be created from aquarium tanks, large brandy snifters, or glass bowls, or you can construct one of glass and wood. Shop around for an attractive container in which to create an unusual terrarium. A cover of glass should be provided, or a cover can be improvised with plastic wrap or some other material. Some terrariums can be left open, but you must be certain to check more frequently for watering requirements.

Large terrariums can be used to freshen potted plants in their containers, or they can be planted or even landscaped with hills, trees, pools, or a waterfall. Use your creativity and imagination.

Planting: Air in a terrarium stays humid, as in a greenhouse, so the climate is ideal for a variety of house plants, tropicals, and semi-tropicals. Choose young, slow-growing plants that won't crowd one another. Seedling-sized plants are easy to obtain and work well in terrariums.

Leaving the plants in their pots will limit their growth and allow you to move them around or thin them without disrupting the whole planting. Place the largest plants first, then add bark, peat moss, or soil. Then arrange the smaller plants and cover the pots with soil—just up to, but not covering, the base of the stems. Wet the plants and the surrounding material. Water condensation on the glass each night will indicate moisture inside. Remove the cover to allow some of the moisture to escape. Don't water again until the soil feels almost dry; this may not be for several months.

Moss can be placed next to the glass so that the soil will not be visible from the outside. Fluorescent lights can be used effectively to aid growth of plants in terrariums (see chapter on Fluorescent Light Gardening, pages 84-89).

Plants for Terrariums: Many plants are adaptable for growing in terrariums. Experiment, find out what does well for you. Try African violets, ferns, moss, small orchids, small philodendrons, ivy, begonias, palms (small), peperomias, fittonia.

SNIFTER makes delightful terrarium. This one is ¼ full of vermiculite.

PLACE plants in position. After planting, water well. Makes decorative display.

YEAR-AROUND GUIDE

JANUARY

Adjust watering schedule to compensate for house heat. Raise humidity by the use of pebble-filled trays. Spray foliage once or twice a day if leaves are not hairy. At night protect plants from cold windows. Light may be insufficient now, resulting in leggy growth. Don't overwater. Use little or no fertilizer, for the growth rate is slow anyway unless plants are grown under artificial lights.

Branches of forsythia, quince, pussy willow, and other early-blooming shrubs can be brought in and forced into bloom.

FEBRUARY

Same general care is needed as in January. Propagate by air layering dieffenbachia, rubber plant, dracaena, fatsia, fatshedera. Prune hibiscus, geraniums—keep plants on dry side after pruning.

MARCH

Plants start making good growth. Air-layered plants should be ready for potting. If you have additional plants that would profit by air layering, do it this month. Make leaf cuttings of African violets, peperomias, Rex begonias. Move plants from strong midday sunshine or shade them slightly. Check plants to see if they need repotting. Topdress with new potting soil those that don't need repotting.

APRIL

Start regular fertilizing program—half strength, once a week. Pot all well rooted cuttings. Keep plants watered; newly potted or severely pruned plants should be kept a little drier. Start tubers of gloxinias, caladiums.

MAY

Plants should be looking much better now that there is less artificial heat and longer days provide better light. Less water should be needed, but keep a constant check. Newly potted plants should be watered sparingly, given extra humidity, and not fed until new growth is in evidence. Continue fertilizing other plants. Repot seedlings as necessary.

JUNE-JULY

Plants should look good now. Repot smaller plants if they need it. Spray leaves with forcible jets of water to keep them clean and to reduce pest incidence.

Plants may be moved outdoors. If you intend to sink pots in the ground, place some drainage material in the bottoms of the holes. Pick a cloudy day and situate plants according to their cultural needs.

AUGUST

Lift plants that have been buried to be sure they haven't rooted outside of the pot. Fertilize all root-filled pots. Watch for insects.

SEPTEMBER

Winter will be coming soon, so prepare plants for the house. Remove dead leaves; clean plants with a wet sponge. Check for pests, and treat if any are present. Bring plants in the house at least two weeks before house heat goes on. Plant bulbs in pots for early spring flowering inside. Taper off watering of tubers and allow them to go dormant. Store when dry.

OCTOBER

Make adjustments in watering schedule if necessary because of house heat. Prepare trays of stones; syringe leaves. Don't overwater cactus and succulents, but don't let them dry out completely. Rest Christmas cactus from October to mid-November by giving them little or no water; keep them cool.

NOVEMBER

Routine care is required for plants in the house this month. Don't overwater. Fertilize (lightly) only plants with large leaves and potbound plants. Move plants away from cold windows, or draw a drape. Keep plants away from radiators or heat source. Give plants all possible sunlight now. Long, spindly growth indicates poor light—supplement with artificial light if possible.

DECEMBER

Wash large-leaved plants with soapy water and sponge—this will open dust clogged stomata. Watch for growth on amaryllis; when growth appears, topdress or repot, and water. Bring into a sunny spot. Keep hoya dry and cool; start to water Christmas cactus, and bring them into a warm, sunny room. Watch that terrariums don't overheat. Keep gift plants away from drafts. Bring potted bulbs in if roots are showing in drainage hole. Leave in complete darkness for a week to induce longer stems. Place hyacinths in light when shoots are 5 inches tall, tulips and narcissus when 3 inches tall.

SMALL CUTTING of jade plant is set in needle holder in water. Cutting will root and can be potted.

PORTULACARIA becomes focal point with addition of slim tapers and Mexican straw angels.

ECHEVERIA ELEGANS planted in concrete bowl in tree pattern is outlined with candles.

ARALIA, simply decorated with gold balls, makes an elegant holiday plant. This one is in 14-inch pot.

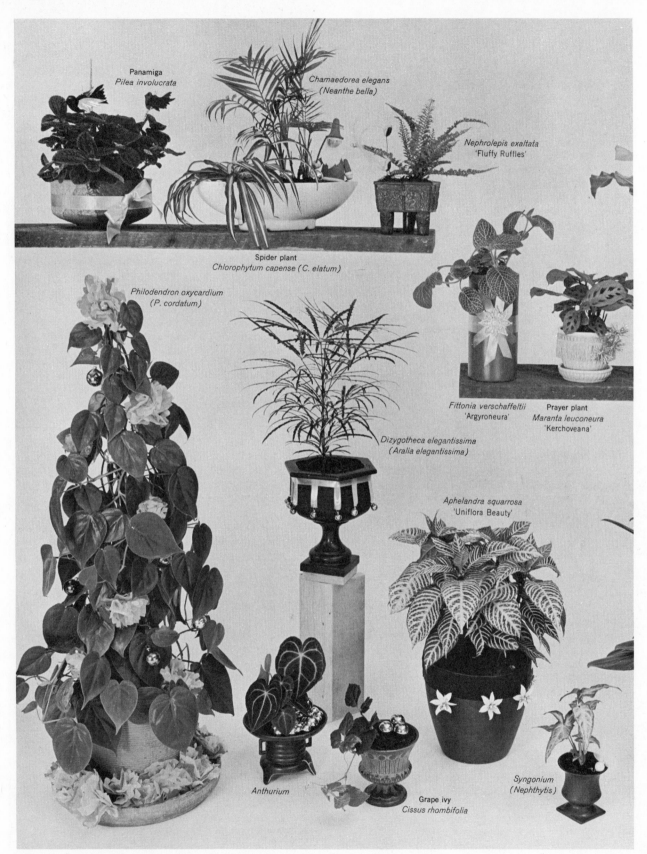

Panamiga
Pilea involucrata

Chamaedorea elegans
(Neanthe bella)

Nephrolepis exaltata
'Fluffy Ruffles'

Spider plant
Chlorophytum capense (C. elatum)

Philodendron oxycardium
(P. cordatum)

Fittonia verschaffeltii
'Argyroneura'

Prayer plant
Maranta leuconeura
'Kerchoveana'

Dizygotheca elegantissima
(Aralia elegantissima)

Aphelandra squarrosa
'Uniflora Beauty'

Anthurium

Grape ivy
Cissus rhombifolia

Syngonium
(Nephthytis)

LEAF AND FORM variation make each plant a showpiece in the right place. Use plants as gifts or to decorate your own home. Tissue paper flowers decorate philodendrons.

If you received a plant for Christmas or for some other special occasion, it should be given special attention to be kept in good condition. Here are some suggestions:

First remove foil that is wrapped around the pots, or poke holes through it so that the water doesn't collect at the bottom. Give plants as much light as possible, but keep them out of direct sunlight to prevent foliage from burning. Rotate plants so that all sides get equal amounts of light. Don't place plants near a heater or fireplace or in a drafty spot.

Outdoor plants should go out as soon as possible. Camellias, holly, pyracantha, living Christmas trees, and other outdoor plants won't thrive in warm, dry household air. Plant them, or at least set them outside, as soon as the weather permits. Plant roses and other bare-root plants as soon as you can. If you can't do this right away, keep the roots constantly moist by covering them with wet sawdust, peat moss, soil, or other material.

Florist plants can remain in the house all the time you are enjoying their blooms. But most of them should go outside at some point later on. Here are instructions for keeping them flowering and caring for them when bloom is over:

Azaleas: Most of the azaleas people receive at holiday time are grown in greenhouses and forced to bloom ahead of season. With good care they will continue to bloom for as long as three or four weeks indoors.

Put plants in the coolest room in the house. Keep soil constantly moist but never soggy. (Watch soil carefully, since it often tends to dry out quickly.) Pinch off old flowers as they fade. When the plants finish blooming, move them into the garden to a spot that gets partial shade all day or sun in the morning, shade in the afternoon. Plant in a soil mix containing at least half peat moss, ground bark, or other organic matter. Or move the plants into slightly larger containers—but keep them outdoors. Feed with acid fertilizer. Given this treatment, the azaleas will get back on schedule and bloom in the spring.

A note as to the hardiness of azaleas should be helpful. The Belgian Indicas are hardy to 20°-30°. Kurumes on the other hand are hardy from 5°-10°. If you live where winters are below these ranges, your azaleas will not survive.

Florists' cyclamen: These need more coolness than do azaleas. Put them on a porch or patio or in some other cool spot, and they may keep blooming until Easter. If kept indoors, the plants sometimes look wilted during the day—more likely the result of warm, dry air than lack of water. Don't overwater.

When plants stop blooming, pull off yellow leaves and stems. Then you have the choice of setting plants out in the garden or keeping them in containers.

Planting in the garden: Choose a spot that gets direct sun only in the morning or filtered sunlight all day. Plant in soil containing about two-thirds organic matter. Don't bury the corm (the knobby bulblike part). When a new growth starts, feed twice a month with liquid fertilizer.

Keeping in a container: Place pot outdoors in exposure recommended above—either set it on top of the ground or (to reduce maintenance) sink it into the ground. Cut down on watering, but never let the corm dry out completely. When new growth starts in the fall, water more often and begin fertilizing. The cyclamen should bloom again the next winter.

Kalanchoe blossfeldiana: This is one plant that can stay in the house all year, but it does grow better and is more likely to bloom again the next Christmas if you put it outside after the last frost in the spring. Water carefully; then let the soil dry out before watering again. Don't let water splash and stain foliage. Feed with light applications of complete fertilizer at monthly intervals. When plants are through blooming, cut off old flower stalks and cut back any leggy stems.

Poinsettias: These plants are especially sensitive to drafts and overwatering—either causes leaves to drop. Don't water until soil starts to dry out. Do not let water stand in the saucer underneath.

When plants stop blooming, move them to a cool, dark place, such as a garage. Reduce watering. Cut plants back part way, so that each stem is left with two buds. In late spring, put them outdoors. You can leave plants in their containers, but by the next Christmas they will probably be too tall to bring indoors. Also, poinsettias are easier to grow in the ground.

In frost-free areas, poinsettias grow and bloom without any trouble right out in the open. In areas where temperatures occasionally go below 32°, they need overhead protection to survive through the winter. It is best to plant them against a sunny, south-facing wall.

Citrus: These plants vary in height from a few inches to 3 or 4 feet; the fruits also vary in size. All have attractive evergreen foliage and fragrant, creamy white flowers that may be produced off and on throughout the year.

The little citrus plants need sun in the wintertime. The plants will do best near a south or west-facing window, in a room where the temperature can be kept constant at between 60° and 70°. Fertilize regularly.

After the weather begins to warm up, the plants will benefit from an hour or two outdoors on sunny days. Showers will be beneficial for the plants. Indoors, give plants a fine water spray once a week.

INDEX

Boldface numbers refer to photographs

PHOTOGRAPHERS

William Aplin, pages: 27 (bottom left), 45 (bottom left), 62 (all 3 photos), 65 (bottom left); **Nancy Bannick,** pages: 27 (top right), 79 (bottom left); **Ernest Braun,** pages: 10 (bottom right), 11 (top right), 12, 21 (bottom), 24 (bottom left), 39 (botton left), 43, 46 (top right); **Tom Burns, Jr.,** page: 86 (top); **Glenn M. Christiansen,** pages: 20 (bottom), 21 (top), 42 (right), 44, 45 (top left, right), 49 (bottom right), 61 (top left), 92 (top right, bottom left), 93; **Richard Dawson,** pages: 6, 13 (top left), 42 (left), 48; **Dearborn-Massar,** page: 10 (bottom left); **Richard Fish,** pages: 13 (right), 30, 41 (top); **Tatsuo Ishimoto,** page: 47 (top); **Roy Krell,** page: 35 (bottom); **Ells Marugg,** pages: 20 (top), 23, 24 (bottom right), 27 (bottom right), 67 (bottom left), 72, 73, 74, 79 (bottom right); **Jack McDowell,** pages: 7 (bottom right), 8 (left, bottom right), 10 (top left), 11 (top left), 75 (bottom); **Rod McLellan Co.,** pages: 68, 77 (top right); **D. Charles Moffat,** pages: 8 (top right), 9, 36; **Don Normark,** pages: 7 (top, bottom left), 10 (top right), 11 (top right), 17, 19 (left), 24 (top), 25, 26, 28 (top), 31 (top), 32, 34, 35 (top), 37, 39 (right), 41 (bottom), 46 (bottom right), 54, 56 (bottom), 58 (bottom right), 85, 86 (bottom); **Roy Pesch,** pages: 46 (top left), 58 (bottom left), 66 (right), 67 (bottom left), 79 (top); **John Robinson,** pages: 18, 19 (right); **Blair Stapp,** page: 90; **Hugh N. Stratford,** page: 46 (bottom); **Paul V. Thomas,** pages: 13 (bottom left), 28 (bottom); **Darrow M. Watt,** pages: 4, 14, 15, 22, 27 (top left), 29, 31 (bottom), 33, 38, 39 (top left), 40, 49 (top left, bottom left), 50, 51, 52, 53, 55, 56 (top), 57, 58 (top left), 60, 61 (right, bottom left), 64 (bottom), 65 (top, bottom right), 66 (left), 67 (top left, bottom right), 69, 75 (top), 76, 77 (top left, bottom), 78 (top), 80, 88, 89, 92 (top left, bottom right); **Steve C. Wilson,** pages: 46 (bottom left), 59.

Art work by **Deborah Neve.**